THE MIRACLE BOOK

A boy and his Bible

by Robert Hicks

A special Christmas limited edition 2003

Limited edition published in Great Britain in 2003
by 'Creative Publishing' Downwood, Bath, BA2 6DT

*All Bible quotations are taken from the Authorised (King James) Version
unless otherwise stated.*

Abbreviations:

GNB – Good News Bible

JB – Jerusalem Bible

NIV – New International Version

Designed by Steve Carroll

Illustrations by Annabelle Hicks

Printed in India

ISBN 086347 5922

CONTENTS

THE MIRACLE BOOK

The Robert Hicks' story, to many observers, is a remarkable tale of 'rags to riches' – although the accumulation of riches for personal use is not part of Robert's makeup.

The childhood experiences of Robert are recalled in "A Child Cries".

"The Miracle Book" describes the lifeline that became first an educational bridge and then a spiritual path into the wider world. In many ways, this is a 'dip in' book.

The first chapters deal with Robert's escape from an horrendous childhood, made more wretched by his being both severely tongue-tied and dyslexic. This meant he spent his first fifteen years as virtually a prisoner within his own mind. Following a successful operation on his tongue, the surgeon suggested that he might wish to copy out a book for education. Robert's search for a suitable book, led to his discovery of the only book in the house: a 350-year-old translation of the Bible.

Robert's copied out that Bible as a means of education, but this process led him to realise that it was in fact his "Miracle Book" and it set him free in so many different ways.

This "Miracle Book" became a guide for life and its impact was seen later when Robert's wife Joyce was diagnosed with cancer and Robert and his children had to deal with bereavement.

Three other sections of the book follow:

1. "A Child's Thoughts" contain a collection of raw expressions from Robert's mind as a child. Through them you can see the emotions he was going through and his perception of the world.

2. A beautiful account of the healing properties of nature, which were part of Robert's childhood experience.

3. A selection of what Robert has called, "Miracle Words". Here are 365 quotations from the Bible, mostly taken from the old translation he used as a boy.

Thoughts about Robert Hicks

Thoughts from Joanna Hicks, daughter

Looking back on my childhood, although I was aware of my father's love and concern for all his children, I realised I had a Dad who found it difficult to show me affection in the conventional way of hugs and kisses, as well as in verbal expressions. In time, of course, I realised that there is very little about my Dad that is conventional!

One of the many memories we all have, is the amount of time he gave to us, even though he worked long hours plus a further hour travelling by tube out of London. One way I can describe this is that, on many occasions, he would come home from work - undoubtedly tired and exhausted - and find all four of us children already in bed. He always came straight upstairs to engage us in one of his magical adventure stories which would captivate our imagination. From downstairs, we would hear the regular shout from our Mom, "Bob, your dinner's getting cold!" Eventually, the voice from downstairs would call, "Bob, your dinner is cold!"

Anyone who knows my Dad would confirm that he is hopeless at anything practical. He wouldn't even know how to wire up a plug, let alone put a fuse into it. 'DIY' is a completely foreign language to him.

However, when it comes to advice of any nature, he always shows great insight and although he does not push his ideas forward in a demanding way, in the longrun, I have regretted the times I have chosen not to follow his suggestions.

I know that I speak also on behalf of my elder sister and brothers in saying that we have a Dad we are extremely proud of. He has always been there for me, especially through some very difficult times in my own life.

As I get closer to my Dad and feel secure in his love and availability to me, I realise that while he can be a best friend, he is a complex individual and there are many sides to his makeup. He has lived in the hard places where I and many have not been. I suspect he has overcome numerous obstacles throughout his life and I am so proud, extremely proud, of who he is and that he is always there for me.

Thoughts from Jeannette Hicks, older sister

I wish there was a lot I could say about my brother Bobby in his childhood years, but the truth is that all of us children were so busy trying to survive and escape from our unnatural and wicked home life, that we had little time to observe each other.

Also, we were constantly being taken into so-called 'care' within Institutions in different parts of the country.

However, I do have very clear memories that my younger brother Bobby was a very quiet child, always thinking and always keeping his thoughts to himself.

He was so quiet that, most times, we did not even know whether he was there! He also spent a lot of time – as we all did – keeping as far away from home as possible, roaming the farmland that surrounded us at that time.

Then, when Bobby started work, it all changed. He was always writing in his corner of the small living room, using the wooden cover that hid the gas meter as his desk. He started educating himself by copying out the Bible by hand. His powers of concentration were incredible and he spent hour after hour copying the text which at the beginning he could not read for himself.

I am pleased that Bobby has now told the story through his own eyes of those terrible years at 335 Stonehouse Lane. After talking to me about the abuse and ordeals I suffered at the hand of my father and the fear for my life that he instilled into me, I wanted Bobby to include this in his book. I realise now that I was not to blame, though for many years my life was damaged so much that, from time to time, suicide seemed the only possible escape. Of course it would not have been!

I do hope that Bobby's story will be read by many and that, in the process, children even today who are threatened by adults close to them, might find genuine friends who can protect and save them from the many torments that we as a family had to endure.

Of course, I am very proud of my brother Bobby and though he often says that I am the real hero of the family, no-one can dispute that – considering the home background from which we came and the lack of education and his own speech and dyslexia handicaps, what he has achieved is marvellous. However, I am even more proud of who he has turned out to be, rather than all those other achievements.

Thoughts from Bernard Hicks, younger brother

I am looking at a photograph of my younger brother, Brian, standing below an oil painting of my elder brother Bobby which now hangs at the entrance to the huge students' library at Birmingham University.

As I look at the portrait of Bobby which – was painted by Mr. Henry Mee, the distinguished portraiter of royalty, captains of industry and other celebrities – I find it amazing that my brother should be there at all!

He left school at fifteen and his first job was normally an occupation for schoolboys; delivering groceries on the old-fashioned bicycles with a large basket on the front. He was an errand boy.

As children, we did not view school as a place for education. But it was important as a place of warmth and shelter in winter, a place to get clean in the regular showers, a place to get free milk and a place to keep hunger at bay with the free dinner system which then operated.

With the free dinners, we always ate as much as we could, because many times that would have to last until the next school day, other than possibly a slice of bread with lard for breakfast – and even that was not always available.

Home was a prison, a dreadful prison, which destroyed all our childhoods. It was not surprising that we would run wild across the open fields belonging to the farms, making dens in trees and under bushes, jumping brooks, riding horses bareback, playing around the 'clay pits' – deep stale water hiding all sorts of rubbish – but we would still jump in and paddle our way around. Bobby has told about those times in his book.

Immediately he had his operation for his speech problem, Bobby began to copy out the Bible. His wild days in the fields were then over. From that moment, slowly but surely, his life was changed and he became focussed in everything that he did.

For most of our life, even as children, we were separated from each other, being constantly transferred from one Institution to another, in different parts of the country.

It is only now, after our families have grown up, that we are beginning to appreciate each other and also realise how much we were robbed by both our parents. This is a sobering thought for all of us who have brought children into the world.

If the thousands and thousands of students who visit the library at Birmingham University were to discover the story of the early years of the mature man they see in the portrait, I am sure they would be motivated to put to good use the privileges and gifts that have come their way and also would want to help the under-privileged who have so much less.

We are all very proud of our brother Bobby and hope that his story is read and appreciated by many people.

Thoughts from Brian Hicks, youngest brother

Bobby was as wild as all of us. We tried to keep as far away a we could from Dad and his bad ways.

If we were not out of the house when he woke up from his 'boozing', we would become his slaves throughout the day and at night time we always dreaded being turned into his 'punchbags' when he was in one of his violent drunken moods.

We all went to Institutions for various reasons. In my case, at one time I ran away and slept rough in the fields for seven days and nights. Because of that, I was sent from 335 where I suffered physical abuse, to an Institution of regimental discipline. We never found human love in our childhood.

Bobby was definitely the quiet one of the family and he was always thinking. Looking back, I realise that there were leadership qualities in him, some of which are reflected in his stories.

Bobby also was hardworking, which is why he succeeded in business, but it was impossible for us as children – or even as adults – to realise that Bobby would be so successful in so many different ways.

I am sure that anyone who reads Bobby's story for themselves will be as surprised as we are in his own family!

Thoughts from Bethany Chapel, Prenton, Wirral

During his time as a member of Bethany Chapel, Prenton, Birkenhead, Bob Hicks was an inspirational Bible teacher.

In his childhood, Bob had turned a speech impairment problem into an advantage by copying and understanding large sections of the Scriptures. From those early days, his love for the Bible was established and, his infectious enthusiasm for God's Word was caught by those who were taught by him.

His notoriety soon extended beyond his local church and he was much sought after across Wirral and Merseyside for his ministry and teaching. He excelled in commencing Bible projects such as compact 'Bible Schools'. He was also a founder member of the 'Way for Wirral' tent crusades and organised a period of practical experience for over 100 students from 'Capernwray Hall' to work alongside a dozen churches in their communities. More recently, Bob's presentation of "The Big Picture" – a complete overview of the Bible in word and song – has proved to be a blessing to many churches and their congregations.

We commend him for the strong Biblical foundation of his faith and his highly developed and innovative skills as a Bible teacher allied to his long experience of Christian work and service.

The Elders of Bethany Chapel, Prenton:

Brian Bagot	John Fletcher
Mal Kendrick	David Ost
Tim Parkinson	Steve Spence
Alan Watson	Les Wootton

Thoughts from Aubrey Marks

Bob - A Person full of Surprises

I invited Bob Hicks to be the Guest Speaker at the celebration of the Golden Wedding for myself and my wife Sheila.

You can imagine my surprise to discover that the following week he would be making a presentation at Buckingham Palace for Her Majesty the Queen during the celebrations of her Golden Jubilee!

The reason for visiting Buckingham Palace was to present a Commemoration Jubilee Bible – the same text that Bob Hicks had copied out in his teens in order to educate himself.

I know that seems incredible, but when Bob Hicks left school – beside being homeless, he was unable to read, write or speak properly, and the only job available to him was as a humble grocery boy for a Family Grocer.

The reason for this was not only his disadvantaged background, but also he was handicapped by being both dyslexic and tongue-tied.

However, I have said that Bob is full of surprises.

Following successful surgery on his tongue, in his fifteenth year, he was determined to learn to read and write and speak correctly. He achieved this by copying out the only book that was available to him: the 350-

year-old translation of the Bible, known affectionately as the "AV" (Authorised Version).

Owing to the fact that I was the Regional Sales Manager for a large dairy product supplier, I was in the right position to witness the transformation of – in human terms – this 'reject of society' becoming a happily married man and Manager of one of the most aggressive Supermarkets in the UK at that time.

Bob's marketing skills were well known by not only my Dairy Company, but also numerous other companies. He achieved successes, which various manufacturers found it difficult to keep up with!

When, eventually, he left the Midlands and moved to the North-West, I contacted his Regional Director enquiring why he had let such a good man go. I will always remember his response, "Yes, he was one of our best Managers, but he was so far ahead in marketing that we couldn't control him!"

Through friends in the North-West, I also heard of Bob's exploits when he took on the responsibility of Marketing Director of over 110 retail shops of all sizes as well as opening the first out-of-town hyper-store which in itself was a great achievement as he had no references to draw upon. Today, it is ASDA Superstore, which belongs to the giant USA retailers 'Wal-Mart'.

During that time, I heard how he was co-Founder of a 5-year Christian Tent Crusade called "Way for

Wirral", as well as organising Spring and Autumn Bible Schools. If that were not sufficient, he also arranged for over 100 students from different parts of the world who were studying at Capernwray Hall to gain some practical experience in working alongside churches in their community.

Were more surprises to come? Yes, there were!

At the height of his career in retailing, he decided to move his family to London in order to become a 'publisher'. You may well ask, "Was this the same boy who could not read or write, now believing he could succeed in publishing?"

Over the years, Bob Hicks founded various publishing companies, some secular, some Christian, and has shaped up marketing-wise publishing companies in the UK, Europe and the United States.

To illustrate: one of his projects was to bring together three publishers (two in the UK and one in the USA) and with a team (one of whom is now a Bishop) to create a multi-media Bible for children. This resulted in the 'Ladybird Bible' from the world-famous children's publishers, numerous individual books of the Bible, a 24-part TV series and an audio-visual presentation for schools and churches.

In more recent days, one of the major initiatives for the Millennium Celebrations was the 'Millennium Bible Gospels', which ran into many millions of copies, distributed not only in the UK but in various languages into 'developing countries'.

There are even more surprises to come! Bob has been invited by Trans World Radio to be involved behind the microphone. He feels that a new opportunity has opened up that could be a blessing to many, especially in 'developing countries'.

Now, I have only highlighted a few surprises in the life of Bob Hicks. However, I am the first to acknowledge that I know very little about what happened before he emerged from the dark shadows of a life that no child should have to endure.

Now that a door has been opened into those early tragic years of Bob's life, I am confident it will be an inspiration to many; especially to those who are burdened by a broken childhood and as a reminder to those who enjoyed a happy childhood of how grateful they should be.

I know Bob Hicks today as an encourager to many, a family man and – of course – a successful man in more ways than one. However, Bob would be the first to acknowledge the goodness of God in his life.

I can only stand back and acknowledge that such achievements were made possible by a power outside of himself – namely God.

I have no hesitation in commending the story of Bob Hicks to you all.

Thoughts from Henry Evans

A Boy Called Bob

I am now in my eighties and, over the years, have had the privilege of working in many youth groups within the church, and in Bible studies at home.

Amongst all those young people, there emerged a young boy – as if he had jumped straight out of the pages of 'Dickens'!

This boy emerged from a dark, broken background – but, once free from his childhood, burst on the scene with such energy, enthusiasm and sensitivity that I, with others, prayed earnestly that he would put it to good use for the benefit of others.

This was a boy whose past was a mystery, except that we all knew it had been horrendous.

When this boy came to our home Bible studies, I was embarrassed for him as he was unable to read or speak correctly However, in spite of that embarrassment, he would volunteer and try hard to be part of the group.

I realised he was a 'born leader' as other young men gathered round him. This boy was always in the front!

Over the years, I have come to know this 'boy' and bear witness to the miracles that took place in his life. Whatever he did – with the boundless energy that was within him – he turned it into success. Against incredible obstacles, he rose again and again, reached new heights, involved himself in new initiatives, succeeded in both retailing and publishing and became involved in the lives of so many from all walks of life because of his love for the Bible and people.

Then, at the height of his powers, tragedy struck again and his wife was taken away from him, far too young, which meant he had to face bereavement and build his life all over again.

Of course, that 'boy' is now Bob Hicks, who is loved and respected by so many.

For myself, the verse from the 'Good Book' that comes to mind – and has come to my mind many times when thinking of Bob Hicks – is that he is a 'vessel, chosen of God'.

To me, it appears that, from the most tragic of situations, God again and again performs His greatest miracle. I believe that Bob Hicks is such a miracle.

To those of us who have known Bob from his mid-teens, we have witnessed God's goodness in his life. The millions of Bibles, New Testaments and Bible Gospels that have been distributed all over the world serve to highlight just one aspect of his life. However, except for a few snippets, those first fifteen years have remained a mystery to us. Now, with this book, light has shot into those hidden early days and I, for one, in my eighties, am pleased to read of those days, dark and difficult though they are, in which God Himself was working.

I know that Bob himself would be the first to say that even in those difficult days, though he did not realise it at the time, he was not alone.

My prayer is that all those who read Bob's story would reach the same conclusion for their lives, whether difficult or less so – they are not alone.

So, from a man in his eighties, looking back to a boy in his teens, I can only praise God for the way he has used that uneducated, deprived, unloved, unwanted boy, who in his early years could not communicate to the outside world, yet after the operation to release him from his speech impediment, discovered the Holy Scriptures which became his educational and guide book for life, the true 'Miracle Book' if ever there was one.

Thoughts from Paul Marsh

I have known Robert now for over thirty years and, during that time, our friendship and my respect for him and his skills have grown.

Anyone who knows Robert professionally, will know that he is an easy man to love, but a difficult man to keep up with!

When we first interviewed him at Scripture Union for the position of 'Marketing Director', I was struck with the multiple successes that he had already achieved in retailing and the incredible enthusiasm and energy he was bringing to Scripture Union.

My only fear was whether that enthusiasm could be channelled through such a traditional institution as Scripture Union then was.

Within weeks, we experienced what Tony Capon described in an article in the "Daily Telegraph" as 'a hurricane'. At that time, at Scripture Union, we had an ever-increasing mountain of unsold books which were a drain on our financial resources as well as not achieving the purpose for which they had been published. Robert did something unbelievable! He made arrangements for all the books to be returned to the printers, and have their covers removed, then replaced with new colourful covers. He packed them as multi-packs within slip cases under new brands and then increased their sale price to reflect the current prices of other publishers! The childrens books were given brand names of animals: Leopards, Tigers, Giraffes, as well as an Inspector Detective Series and a Treasure Chest series. Robert sold these to W H Smith as well as the Christian Book Trade. This was just the beginning ...

However, it was something of a 'bumpy ride' for Scripture Union, because Robert clearly set out that he had little time for the 'committee-structure' involving series of meetings and a long haul to reach any decision – which was the way movements like Scripture Union had been traditionally run.

Tom Houston, then the General Secretary of 'The Bible Society' told Robert that he expected him to last two years in the job – and that was meant as a compliment! Edward England, the renowned publisher at "Hodders" said that Robert was "The best thing that had happened in the Christian book scene for years." David Alexander, the much loved (now sadly missed) publisher at Lion Publishing used a more descriptive expression when he said, "Robert Hicks has given us all a kick up the backside!"

Well, Robert stayed well beyond the predicted two years and we worked together very closely. He respected my editorial skills as I respected his entrepreneurial creative and marketing ones.

While at Scripture Union, Robert could see potential for a huge publishing operation, but believed this would only materialise if the retail shops and publishing were a separate division from Scripture Union's traditional role as a missionary movement. He predicted (in his normal, direct way) that if this did not happen, the movement would need to move out of

London, dispose of its shops and lose a large part of its publishing operation.

With such strong convictions, it was understandable that it was only a matter of time before Robert would move on. The various publishing companies he has founded since then speak for themselves and need no comment from me.

I know that Robert is the first to acknowledge his huge debt to Scripture Union and he continues to speak fondly of them and is always encouraged every time he hears of their success and progress.

When Robert's wife Joyce died, I was in Switzerland. Robert wanted me to speak at the funeral thanksgiving service. Without hesitation, I flew back, because of the bond of love I had for Robert and for Joyce and all the family.

As you would expect, from time to time, we talked about Robert's childhood, but there is so much about those difficult days that I don't know. I am pleased that, at last, he has followed the encouragement of Gilbert Kirby, past Principal of the London Bible College, who a long time ago encouraged Robert to write his story, believing it would inspire and motivate others, and I believe the same.

Today, I am not surprised when I hear that Robert has visited Buckingham Palace, or that he is regularly behind the microphone for Trans World Radio, or that he involved in new and exciting projects. That is just the kind of person whom, over the years, I have come to know: a dedicated enthusiast who has a way of making things happen.

Thoughts from Stan and Muriel Purshouse

When Robert, Joyce and their three young children joined our church in the West Midlands, they brought to us a valued vitality and vigour. At the time, Joyce was expecting their fourth child, a daughter, who is now herself a mother of three.

The Hicks Family came just at the right time! A number of teenage girls had recently become Christians and they found a homely welcome – along with other youngsters – at the home of Robert and Joyce. Here they were not only entertained socially, but became part of a Young People's Bible Study Group. One of those young girls recently said that she was "Discipled on Romans" at the Hicks' home.

The time came when these young people, new to the Christian faith, were baptised. I remember that Robert was thrilled when we invited him to perform some of the baptisms.

The leadership of our church had no hesitation in inviting Robert to be a Deacon and, in that capacity, he initiated his first mini-Bible School, working with Tom Dick who eventually became the General

Secretary of S.A.S.R.A. Together, they worked out a programme in which all the leaders would take part, as well as other church members. Robert's love for the Bible and enthusiasm for it was contagious.

We were pleased to hear that, when the family moved to the Wirral, before long there were more Bible Schools taking place, as well as other exciting initiatives. Robert tells me that the basis of those Bible Schools formed the structures that eventually became "Open Home: Open Bible" the 60-part TV-Video series, hosted by Rev. Richard Bewes of All Souls Church in London, in discussion with guests from various parts of the world.

However, attention should not just be given to Robert. His wife Joyce also left her imprint on us, with her energetic enthusiasm and hospitable nature. She is still fondly remembered today as the founder and initiator of a meeting point for women called "Homemakers" which has recently celebrated its 30th Anniversary. Sadly, Joyce could not be at those celebrations as we had to say goodbye to her far too young when she was diagnosed with terminal cancer in her '40's'.

One day, to our surprise, Robert contacted us to say he was coming our way and would like us to host an informal supper for mutual friends, including a single young woman called Annabelle! The same year

Stan had the honour of conducting the marriage of Robert and Annabelle. Further excitement followed three years later as we thrilled over the arrival of Emily-Rose.

For all of us, life has changed so much during the many years since we first met. We have stayed in the same place, whilst Robert has progressed from place to place, leaving his mark on both retailing and publishing. We did know that his childhood was difficult and that he had started life severely tongue-tied until an operation after he had left school, but we did not expect to be able to peer into the detail of those early years. Now, like many of you, we can do so by reading "A Child Cries". We hope that, through Robert's story, you will discover that although our birth or childhood experiences do affect us in what we are and think, it is possible to put these experiences to good use in our adult years.

Robert is a good example of a positive attitude to life in the face of apparently unsurmountable obstacles.

Thoughts from Mrs. Vera Wise

Bobby came into our small Gospel Hall at Jiggins Lane one Sunday, looking like a lost and hungry boy, with his unruly hair partly covering his dark brown eyes. But he also came with a big smile on his face, which disguised a tragic childhood.

The ragged clothes he was wearing were held together with crude sewing and string. Instead of shoes, he was wearing old canvas 'plimsolls' that had seen better days long ago.

Our hearts immediately went out to Bobby. That same day, Fred and I invited him back to share our Sunday lunch. Over the next few years, this became a regular pattern.

It took us time to understand Bobby's speech, because he was recovering from an operation on his tongue. However, he made rapid progress and obviously the surgery had been successful..

When Fred sold our greenhouse, he gave Bobby ten shillings (£0.50) from the proceeds and made it clear that this money was for him to buy himself some basic clothing, such as trousers, shirt and shoes. In those days ten shillings would have been enough to buy such things.

Little did we realise how much this gift would affect Bobby. So much so that, when he became successful in business, he would send out millions and millions of Bible Gospels all around the world, in memory of our simple and spontaneous act of Christian love.

Every day, until Fred became seriousy ill and went to Heaven, we used to pray together for Bobby through all the stages of his life, which included his marriage to Joyce and their four children, the painful cancer experience and Bobby's eventual bereavement, then the happy time of Bobby's marriage to Annabelle and the delightful surprise gift of their daughter Emily-Rose.

Yes, we did pray for Bobby and the Lord has definitely answered exceedingly abundantly above all that we were able to ask or even think.

Over the years, when Bobby has talked about his childhood, we have only learned scraps here and there. His enthusiasm was always directed to future projects rather than past hardships.

However, I am pleased that he has now written his story and I am sure it will be an encouragement and help to many who read it.

I am now in my 'eighties', but I am so grateful that all those years ago the Lord allowed Fred and myself, with our daughter Valerie, to have an open home and a welcome table for the uneducated boy who happened to walk into our church – for which we give praise and glory to God.

Thoughts from Lawrence M Stone, Vice President and Publisher of Rutledge Hill Press Nashville, USA.

I have known Robert Hicks for nearly 25 years. He is one of the most creative, passionate and dedicated friends I have.

Bob's creativity is shown in both his ability to market books effectively as well as create books and editions of the Bible and Bible portions.

The words, "we've always done it that way" are not in Bob's vocabulary! He is always searching for new and different ways to reach people – unchurched as well as church members – with the Word of God and encourage them to read it.

He is involved not jut in marketing the books, but in creating them as well. Once, when he was not able to secure pictures he needed at a price he wanted to pay, he decided to create his own photo library – initially with beautiful pictures he took himself. He has a unique ability to think with both an editorial and a marketing focus.

Bob is passionate and single minded, always thinking of new ways to encourage people to read Scripture. He believes strongly that it is the Word of God that will change people's lives and the application of Scriptural truths will enable the believer to rejoice at God's blessings and find help in times of hardship.

Bob is dedicated to the task. He has encouraged the publication and dissemination of Scripture portions and Christian books, not just in England, but in many Third World countries. Millions of portions of Scripture have had the opportunity of changing lives because of the dedication of Robert Hicks. And his ideas are always fresh, innovative and effective.

But, most of all, he is a good and generous friend, always willing to lend a helping hand and an encouraging word.

Thoughts from Vic Mitchell

"The Robert Hicks story is truly an amazing saga. As one who has seen his life develop as a Christian, business man and family man, – overcoming dyslexia, clarity of speech, homelessness and poverty – I can only stand back and acknowledge that such achievements were made possible by a power outside of himself, namely God."

Bob Hicks is a warm-hearted, unique man, from a unique background, possessing outstanding gifts as a visionary, motivator and creative communicator of the Christian message.

Thoughts from Rev. John Walker

Having known Bob in seasons of sadness and joy, I can think of no-one who has overcome adversity in quite the way he has.

From childhood deprivation, struggling to read and write, to a thousand new ideas flowing from his fountain pen before breakfast, Bob has an appetite for the Bible and the God of the Bible, second to none.

Mid-life bereavement and a new family have only served to fuel his desire to communicate the timeless truths of God's Word.

I'm left breathless from being in his company, but always leave him with a fresh desire to become as enthusiastic as he is for his twin passions: God and the Bible.

Thoughts from Rev Dr Steve Brady, Principal, Moorlands College, Christchurch

A first-class honours graduate from the "College of Hard Knocks", Robert exemplifies the Christian principle that 'It's not where you come from that matters, but where you are going that counts!'

Our students at Moorlands College just loved him!

Thoughts from Michael Pfunder, Trans World Radio

Robert Hicks has been a regular guest on TWR's live broadcast, "Good Morning UK". His topical, humorous and compassionate press reviews reflect his love for Scripture and the people who haven't heard its message. Robert is also working on a Bible teaching series, in conjunction with TWR, which is aimed primarily at an overseas audience.

Whenever he gets behind the microphone, Robert combines the timeless Gospel with life in our times, and I look forward to holding a copy of his own life story in my hands.

Thoughts from Martin H Manser, Reference Book Editor, Language Trainer and Consultant

Bob Hicks is an enthusiast. He is an enthusiast for Jesus Christ, for the Bible and for spreading the Christian message in a contemporary way to the world.

Thoughts from ALAN BAIN, Friend and BBC Bristol Producer & Presenter 1998-2001

This was a sad, depressing house to film; heartbreaking. Being myself a Londoner who has viewed human life at its most raw, I have become accustomed to the difficult parts of life, but I do not know how Robert survived all this and at the same time struggled being tongue-tied and dyslexic. If I had not witnessed the filming that day, I would have found his story difficult to believe, and even more difficult to enter into his experiences.

There was one room that Robert did not enter; that was his father's bedroom – "A dark room of bad memories" is how he described it. Still the fear and horror of that place reached from the young child across the years to the adult man, and prevented him from entering.

Following the home filming, we eventually moved on to the Institution which had been "Middlemore Homes" and part of Robert's childhood. The premises are now part of Birmingham University and the then Principal had given permission for the filming. As he showed us round, I learned that – a few weeks earlier – Robert had enjoyed a private meal with the Principal just a stone's throw from the spot where, fifty years earlier, as a deprived bruised and battered boy he had arrived at the Institution and had 'breakfasted' at suppertime on curled-up sandwiches. Then his clothes had been removed, his hair shaved and he had been disinfected in the shower before sleeping in a huge dormitory of army-style beds between white starched sheets.

We filmed inside that dormitory. Where there had once been twenty-two beds for boys, now there are twenty-two computers occupying students from round the world. What a contrast!

Over the past dozen years, I have grown to know Robert. I remember, when he first came into publishing, how he revolutionised a lot of thinking because of his professional marketing approach. I am constantly amazed at the wide range of enterprises he initiates, sponsors and encourages.

However, after the filming at 335 Stonehouse Lane, I realise I am just beginning to understand the man himself.

Robert talks about his "Miracle Book", but I can testify to a human being who is the first to acknowledge his many weaknesses and mistakes throughout life; a genuine full-hearted man who acknowledges the Bible and the God of the Bible who rescued him from a heartbreaking childhood and enabled him to be and to achieve so much in his life.

Heartily, I commend both "A Child Cries" and "The Miracle Book".

Thoughts from Rev. Jonathan Skinner

Robert Hicks is a unique man in many ways.

For a start, his early years were unusual to say the least. He was born during a bombing raid of the

Second World War in the degrading conditions of a Birmingham slum. Very early on, his mother deserted the home and left him to be raised by his less-than-adequate father in squalid conditions that only the poorest of our land have experienced, physical abuse and much worse being part of the package. Such austerity moulded Robert's developing character. Whereas for many, the results would have been stultifying and destructive, because of another 'special factor', they were peculiarly positive.

But before we touch on this 'special factor', which turned such hardship into profound and staggering advantage, there was another particularly unusual and difficult dimension to Robert's younger years. Due to a physical deformity in his mouth, Robert could not speak; and due to some kind of dyslexic condition, he could not read. Yet, even these inabilities were converted into driving forced for success by his other 'special factor'.

During his teens, Robert attempted to overcome his inability with reading and writing by copying out word for word the only book he could find in the house: the Bible. Using the gas meter as a desk, Robert found, as he worked through this great masterpiece, that it began to have a supernatural effect on his life. At every level, Robert's mind and heart began to be redeemed from his conditions. Through the majestic words and inordinately powerful ideas, Bob's thinking began to change – and that 'special factor' began to take root. It was at this time that Robert came to trust in Jesus and become a committed, believing Christian. Alongside this, a friend diagnosed Robert's condition and soon an operation was performed on him so that his tongue became physically untied.

This combination of unique factors produced abilities and a personality that enabled Robert to have a meteoric rise in the commercial world, becoming head of marketing at the Co-op in the north west of England. Later he set up his own publishing business that at one point was one of the largest independent publishing house in the UK. Alongside this, Robert has initiated a whole raft of other businesses – many that should be included in the "Guinness Book of Records".

Robert's personal Christian faith has not only influenced his business world, but has saturated his personality, family life and involvement with his local church. His personal warmth and ability to 'think out of the box' has also enable him to initiate and drive forward a whole host of Christian endeavours, most notably, but not exclusively in the realm of publishing.

The growth out of all the pain and tragedy of the early years, along with the ability to capitalise on the opportunities in later life, has been brought about by

God working through the mot powerful book available: the Bible. The most significant thing to say about Robert Hicks is that he is a man of the Bible.

Thoughts from George Verwer

The facts speak for themselves: millions upon millions of beautifully produced Gospels distributed widely throughout the developing world and in various languages.

When the 'Berlin Wall' came down, nearly one million quality full colour New Testaments, designed in England, printed in Italy and distributed through publishers and churches, were sent to East Germany.

Million of 'Millennium Gospels' – again beautifully produced – were taken up by 10,000 churches throughout the UK and distributed by over 100,000 Christians to over 25% of UK homes – one of the few reminders that we were celebrating 2000 years since the birth of Jesus Christ.

The individual behind all this is Robert Hicks, whose eyes and heart were opened when he entered into partnership with the much-loved and greatly-missed Philip Morris and his work for OM India.

"Until Philip Morris challenged me to the need of India, I was totally unaware that I could make any contribution of significance to the needs of the developing world. Philip changed all of that. For his vision and directness in talking to me, I shall be for ever grateful."

From the early days, Robert has been a friend to OM, encouraging individuals to work alongside us or with us.

"I remember my first contact with OM. It was the winter of 1963 and I was speaking in a small Christian Brethren church. Into the church came two students from what was then called 'Birmingham Bible Institute'. The verse I spoke on was from John's Gospel: "Without me (Jesus), you can do nothing." In order to add drama to the verse, I paraphrased it, placing the emphasis on, "Without me, you are paralysed." The point I was making is that it is possible for Christians to see God working in a marvellous way, yet find themselves paralysed themselves and uninvolved.

After the meeting, the two young men told me they had been challenged by working with a new movement called "OM". I pleaded ignorance, but that ignorance did not last long!

OM was young in those days. Over the years, I have had the privilege of sharing my home with many individuals who felt called in a variety of ways to be part of that great movement, for which I honour God."

Without Individuals like Robert Hicks, movements like OM would be the poorer. I, for one, am inspired by Robert Hicks and his vision for the Word of God and its distribution.

Thoughts Dr. Peter Brierley, Executive Director, Christian Research

I am grateful to have had the privilege of knowing Robert Hicks. He had a terrible start in life, but the fact that he won through shows not just his determination, but a trait of even greater importance – a total unwillingness to give up. He keeps at it and at it, until he gets there.

This has been of enormous importance to him in the rough-and-tumble of the world of business, but indefatigability is not the only criteria of success. Through the seminars on leadership that I take, and analyses made of cultural swings in the nation (which are published), I am aware that another criteria is necessary. It is summed up in the word "vision". Knowing Robert personally and enjoying hospitality at his home, he had proved to be a good "case study"!

A recent Government report indicated that two-thirds of UK households are in debt, one reason for which was suggested as the lack of ability to look ahead. Research we have undertaken on leaders suggests also that only about one-third can think future – a fraction supported by the educational reformer Piaget in the 1970's. There is no doubt that

Robert is in the one-third who can identify the path ahead.

He looks into the future and plans accordingly, With that, comes the courage to take risks. Of course, sometimes there are mistakes, but Robert has the ability to learn from these. Being willing to take risks, make mistakes and learn from them, are key attributes of leaders, whether in the secular world of business or in the faith world of churches.

Robert is also a people person. A people person thinks of teams or partnerships. There is a long list of enterprises in the publishing and media world he has started or with whom he has a successful working relationship. Some of these, for example, are Creative Publishing; Robert Frederick Ltd.; Grandreams; Top Story; Vine's Books; Bible 1st; Christian Book Club; Great Books Direct; Gospel Gifts; Millennium Gospels; Open Home: Open Bible; The Big Picture; Jubilee Fifty .. and so on. This is apart from working with missionary agencies, publishers and manufacturers throughout Europe and beyond!

The long-term view is seen in his investments. Many individuals have wanted to start their own initiatives, but rather like Richard Branson in the secular world, Robert Hicks in the Christian world has come alongside and befriended and invested in deserving people, even though he didn't expect a return for many years. This is another reflection of his people-people nature. If individuals do not immediately succeed, they should be given an opportunity to try and try again – as Robert did.

Robert's Christian faith is foundational to his way of life. This means he exercises a high degree of trust, delegating to people not just the detail but also the vision-making processes - that is, the "why" as well as the "how". Not many people can do this. Even when 'Concorde' was flying, there were few pilots; likewise, there are few today who are willing to aim so high.

Essential to that aim is Robert's following of the teachings of Jesus Christ, especially in the Gospels. Remember the "Daily Telegraph" offering the combined Gospels free and printing an extract from each in its leader column four days in one week? Robert was behind that!

'Concorde' used to fly at 'Mach 2' – twice the speed of sound. To do that, its throttle was kept fully open. So is Robert's "throttle" fully open, all the time, to follow Jesus on the one hand, but to give individuals and ongoing enterprises a chance on the other – keeping at it and at it, until he (and they) get there.

Thoughts from Rev Richard Bewes, All Souls Church, London

I first met Robert and his engaging family when he moved to London to be a publisher, and we soon formed a friendship, out of which came the "Pocket Handbook of Christian Truth" which in more recent days has been turned into the hugely successful TV/Video series, "Open Home: Open Bible".

Before Robert became a publisher, he had a distinctive and successful career in retailing, being one of those individuals who held an integral part in the 'retail revolution' from the late 50's to the early 70's.

What is even more interesting, is that Robert started in the humblest of positions as a 15-year-old errand boy for a family firm of grocers, for the simple reason that, when he left school, he was not able to read, write or speak correctly – not even knowing the letters of the alphabet.

The reason for this went right back to his early childhood. He was born during a bombing raid and became a 'ragamuffin' street boy, living the slums, punctuated by time away in large Institutions for Children, during the many times his mother was giving birth to yet another child – ten children in all!

He was unaware that he had parents or siblings until around the age of six, when one cold December day his mother came to collect him. Within five years, she would desert all the family and not be heard of again for 28 years.

As if that was not hard enough, Robert's father tragically became abusive, which brought hard brutality in the early hours of the morning when he returned home drunk and made excessive demands of his children.

But that was not all. Robert had been born both dyslexic and severely tongue-tied, which accounted for his lack of formal education. I say 'formal', because in those difficult 15 years of his life, Robert developed powers of observation and an understanding of human nature which would be put to good use in both his retailing and publishing careers.

There then came a time when Robert's life was totally changed. After successful surgery on his tongue, Robert copied out by hand the 'Greatest Book in the English Language'. – in order to learn to read, write and speak correctly. The impact of that book on Robert's life caused him to leave his Marketing Directorship in retailing to become a publisher; a publisher who has made his mark internationally in both the Christian and secular publishing worlds.

I once introduced Robert as a "congenial, creative individual" and over the years, I have seen no reason to change that description.

I have no hesitation in commending the story of

those difficult years.

To many, Robert's story will be disturbing, but it will also bring a challenge. Nearer to us than most realise, there are children in need of genuine Christian love, help and encouragement.

I also predict that this book will be an inspiration to many who can identify personally with Robert's childhood, because they themselves were crying in the dark and thought that nobody was listening.

Robert's story – harrowing though it is – demonstrates that 'Someone' is always listening and in sovereignty continues to surprise us all in the way He raises up individuals to be a blessing to many.

Thoughts from Eric A Bell, Chairman & Chief Executive of a major Ford Dealership, North West England 1980-90

I first met Bob Hicks in 1974 when we both became Founder Members of the five-year Tent Crusade called, "Way for Wirral". Sometimes, when you meet people, you immediately have an affinity with them – it was like this when I met Bob and, before long, between our families too.

For the first few years of "Way for Wirral", I was elected Chairman and Bob Hicks took on the responsibility of marketing. At that time, Bob was the Marketing Director of the once-huge operation in the

North-West: The Birkenhead & District Co-operative Society – which had numerous stores stretching from Liverpool right into North Wales. Robert also played a key role in opening up the first out-of-town 'hypermarket' in the UK and continuing as its Director.

Bob's genius for marketing and advertising was put to good use and it was a joy to see his singleminded approach to the task and his confidence in what he was suggesting. It was not long before the headlines in the local newspaper said, "Wirral's Biggest Tent Crusade for Years".

This was followed up by all the participating churches receiving bundles of a uniquely folded leaflet which initially displayed a short message, but when fully opened became a detailed poster! Robert wanted everyone to be involved and in those early years, the sense of "we are all in this together" was undoubtedly the reason we enjoyed the Lord's blessing. They were happy, rewarding, joyful days – and Robert's enthusiasm was part of it.

Beside the Christian work which, in addition to our secular commitments, extended us both, we also found time for our families to meet up, as well as sharing happy games of tennis together, which also led to a great blessing.

One holiday time, our family met a couple of lads

who joined in the tennis. After the holiday, they continued playing tennis with us and Bob with his family also joined in. One evening, after play, Bob told them how he had come to faith in Christ. It was all very well for us telling them the Gospel, but Bob seemed to get right down to their level as he told them his life story. They started attending the "Way for Wirral" Crusade, and both of them came to faith.

It was a great joy for us to know Bob and Joyce and the family. It was our loss when they moved first to London, then to Bath. Over the years, as we kept in touch, we felt great distress in Joyce's long illness and her homecall. Later, we also shared in Bob's joy when the time came for us to meet up with Bob and Annabelle and their delightful daughter Emily-Rose.

Anyone who knows Bob admires his fortitude and appreciates that he was and is an example of the strength that God gives in time of trouble. His Christian work and commitment to the Bible and Bible distribution, as well as other ventures of faith, are marks of the man. We as a family are pleased that we have grown to know Bob as a person – not just his creativity, marketing and entrepreneurial skills.

The "Way for Wirral" Tent Crusades concluded their five-year mission as we entered into the 1980's, but the work done then still blesses us now on the Wirral and I am thrilled that the Lord, in His goodness, allowed the 'marketing genius of the Co-op' to be with us in those formative years.

BEFORE I START
– WHY THIS BOOK?

It was David Wavre, an experienced Editor and Publisher, and an individual whose judgement I respect, who encouraged me to write this book: Let me tell you why.

The book, "A Child Cries", which covers my first fifteen years, is full of the drama of my life prior to my discovery of the Holy Bible and copying it out. My motive was to overcome my inability to read, write or speak correctly. For the first fifteen years of my life, I was severely tongue-tied as well as being dyslexic.

While I was writing the sequel to "A Child Cries", David was concerned that in the gap between the two books, the readers should be informed of the impact that the Holy Bible made upon me educationally, morally and spiritually, and how it affected what would become my professional life, as well as my family life.

The background events in "A Child Cries" are set against the World War that was taking place in 1941 and up until 1956. It was in 1956 that I discovered the Holy Bible, started copying out by hand, not knowing the impact it would make on my life.

At the time, I was an errand boy, as well as doing odd jobs around the shop, for the well-known family grocers in Birmingham and districts, 'George Mason – The Family Grocer' They had over 30 shops in the midlands, and before the age of 22 I would have managed over half of them.

When I worked over the contents of this book with David, he sympathised with my desire to include in the book a section dealing with my wife's terminal cancer, bereavement and its immediate effect. Fortunately, many cancer sufferers have a happy outcome, but all of us know of a loved one for whom the only happy ending available is what comes after death.

While revisiting my childhood, I have also gathered together some of my inner reflections as "A Child Cries", and these are presented in their raw state. I had numerous thoughts' that circulated constantly in my mind ad a child, for the simple reason that I had no one to communicate them to. I have been advised to leave them without comment.

The 'Miracle Words' section will, I hope, be a useful introduction for many to the 'Miracle Book' itself.

So, this book is now yours! And I hope it will be a real inspiration.

Robert Hicks

THE SURGEON OPERATES

THE SURGEON OPERATES

THE FIRST MIRACLE

I was still fifteen. It was a few months after becoming Errand Boy and doing all the 'odd jobs' around a local branch of "George Mason – The Family Grocer", that the first miracle for me took place in the most ordinary – and yet extraordinary – way.

A divorced nurse, who could no longer work night shifts now that she was without support and solely responsible for her teenage children had taken a position in the same shop where I was working, and was being trained to become a Manageress.

During the 40-minute lunch break, Mrs Siddall – that was her name – spent a few minutes each day encouraging me to spell simple words. However, this proved most unsuccessful, because of a kind of cross wiring of the brain – later diagnosed as 'dyslexia'.

FRUSTRATION

Beside the spelling lessons, she also engaged me in basic elocution because there were so many of the basic language sounds I could not pronounce. I remember very well how often the spelling and elocution sessions would end in frustration for both of us.

ROBERT HICKS

OPEN YOUR MOUTH

Then, one day, something 'clicked' inside Mrs. Siddall's brain and she suddenly and unexpectedly said to me, "Open your mouth and let me look inside!". Then, "I cannot believe it!" she exclaimed, "Your tongue is tied to the floor of your mouth and this is why you are not pronouncing words and why it is so difficult for us to understand you. Poor boy! It's not your fault."

SENSE OF WELL-BEING

Those may not have been the exact words but the kindly sentiments I definitely remember. I also remember a genuine sense of well-being – realising for the first time that I was not to blame for the deficiency and ugliness in the way I tried to express myself.

A HUGE BURDEN

I had lived all those years believing I was something of an idiot and only capable of doing odd jobs around the shop and delivering groceries as an errand boy on those bikes with a large basket carrier on the front. To be free of that responsibility was like a huge burden rolling off my shoulders! Many years later, I would read the famous book "A Pilgrim's Progress" and I could empathise with the exhilaration he felt when he

52

lost his burden at the foot of the cross.

"Bobby, Bobby!" said Mrs. Siddall, "You must promise me that you will go to your Doctor on your way home from work today and let him look into your mouth. This is very important."

Mrs. Siddall made it very clear to me that something could be done, and it needed to be done immediately.

DOCTOR AMAZED

After work, I found myself at the end of a long queue in the Doctor's waiting room. I was happy to be the last person to see him, although I do remember it was a long wait.

I knew Dr. Hutchinson well, although I had never consulted him myself for medical treatment. He was often visiting our house to treat my two brothers – John and Bernard - who suffered with severe asthma.

I think he was surprised to see me at the surgery – but his surprise was greater still when he looked into my mouth. He could not believe it and I remember him expressing his frustration that my parents had not brought this problem to the attention of the Doctor before.

The examination was over in a few moments, performed with a small wooden pallet like a lollipop stick, he was intrigued to see how the back part of my

tongue had developed. There and then, he sat down and wrote in longhand a letter to a surgeon at the huge Selly Oak Hospital, which was in walking distance from the Grocer's shop.

Within two weeks, I was on my way for the operation!

SELLY OAK HOSPITAL

As I was not going to have the operation until the afternoon, I was expected to be at work in the morning. However, I made sure that I borrowed one of John's ties and his shoes and I may even have borrowed one of his shirts. I made my own way alone to Selly Oak Hospital. When eventually I arrived, the Hospital appeared to me as a boy to have miles and miles of corridors, and hundreds of rooms. If the instructions had not been sketched for me on the cover of the envelope, I feel sure I would have been hopelessly lost.

EYES OPEN

Nevertheless, I arrived early and found myself observing numerous individuals in need of medical care of one kind or another.

In many ways, simply going to the Hospital opened my eyes to pain and suffering, and in the faces of others I saw something of the sadness that was going on all around me. Until that time, I had only been aware of the evils taking place at our house, "335", evils that involved all of us as children, but more so for my only sister Jean.

Mother had come into my conscious life when I was six and had left my life within five years and would never be heard of again for another 28 years. Father came into my conscious life when I was seven and crushed it as he did also the lives of all my siblings. Eventually, I fought him, and fought for my freedom on my fifteenth birthday.

There were numerous dramas that had stolen, robbed and indeed killed so much in those precious early years. However, just as I was aware of the poor children in the Institutions to which I was sent from time to time as a child, so I was aware of the great sense of loss and sadness I was witnessing at the Hospital.

A SHOCK

After waiting and watching, the Sister called me and took me in for surgery. She expressed her surprise that I had come alone. Once inside, I had the shock of my life – The surgeon was not alone! Around him stood a group of young men and women all dressed in white aprons who were all going to inspect my mouth and follow the procedure to give my tongue its freedom!

The surgeon – a man who appeared to be in his mid-thirties – was tall and lean and seemed to enjoy explaining to the students what was to take place.

MR. HICKS!

"Mr. Hicks" he said. I should pause here; because this was the first time anybody had addressed me in this way with my surname in a respectful way. At the time, however, this made me feel less adequate and more childish, especially among all these students. These young folk did not look many years my senior, yet there was a huge bridge between us and it would take many years of effort before I felt secure enough to cross over.

"Mr. Hicks, I would like your permission for the students to be present during this operation. I hope you don't mind?"

I nodded my agreement and muttered a soft "Yeth" although deep inside I wished they were not there.

EMBARRASSMENT

The good and kindly surgeon explained to me what would take place. First, he would want me to pronounce to the best of my ability the letters of the alphabet, then he and the student would look into my mouth. He would then 'freeze' my mouth and a little time later he would operate. Then I would be left alone for a couple of hours, but he would return to examine me before I left the hospital.

Even as he was explaining, I was becoming more and more terrified because I did not know the letters of the alphabet!

To my great relief, when the time came for me to make the sounds of the alphabet, the kind surgeon was sensitive to my dilemma and as I began to struggle, he gently said, "Let's start again and you can say the sounds after me. This will give an opportunity for the students to hear the difficulties you have been having up to now."

Slowly the blushing of my face subsided, and somehow we reached the end of that ordeal.

Then came the investigation and numerous questions. Each student in turn with a stainless steel object poked around my mouth. I remember the surgeon pointing out to them – just as my Doctor had observed – the enlarged muscles at the back of my tongue.

I also remember him saying that the membrane should have been cut when I was a young child and the speech difficulties would then never have occurred.

A LIFE-CHANGING QUESTION

However, it was one of the questions from a student that struck me most. It was a male student who raised the question whether there was any connection between my speech difficulties and the spelling problems. I found the surgeon's response interesting.

He said that, in his judgment, the answer was, "Yes." But he believed the main problem was to do with confidence, and the effect that confidence had on motivation. The negative side of being tongue-tied was a lack of confidence, without which it would be difficult to be motivated.

Then came the local anaesthetic, the freezing of the mouth and the operation, which all seemed to pass very quickly. The students thanked me for allowing them to watch and then disappeared.

I was aware that being tongue-tied at this age was rare and that was why the students had been brought in. I remember feeling very sad at being the object of their education in this respect.

The surgeon told me he was pleased with the operation and gave me a time to see him again later. During the long wait, the effect of the anaesthetic gradually diminished and the feeling returned and I was able to drink a warm cup of tea.

AN INSPIRATIONAL INTERVIEW

Eventually, I had the promised interview with the surgeon. He told me that membranes had held down both sides of my tongue and after he had cut them, because they were so tense, they had sprung into small balls beneath my tongue and would remain there throughout my life. True to his word, I can feel them even as I write!

The surgeon then, for a second time, asked me to repeat after him the letters of the alphabet. He told me there was a definite improvement, but what I now needed was professional elocution lessons, which unfortunately were not covered by the Government Health Scheme and therefore would have to be paid for. I indicated that I would try to save up some money for lessons, but unfortunately that never materialised as my Shop Manager, Mr. Hall, was not happy to allow me the time off from work for elocution lessons and discouraged me further by saying he would have to reduce my wages accordingly. At the time, I felt he was being unfair, because I already had a shorter lunch break than the other members of staff because I had to clear up after the shop was closed, as well as staying later in the evenings for the same reason.

There was, however, one piece of advice, which the surgeon gave me, which I was to follow to the letter.

"Mr. Hicks," he said, "if you want to learn to read and write, what I would encourage you to do, is to copy words out by hand and try to pronounce out loud the words you are copying." He also gave me advice about strengthening the muscles at the front of the tongue but what I felt most motivated to do was to find a book and copy it out, and learn to pronounce the words as I went along.

I WAS CURED! – I WAS FREE!

When I came out of the Hospital, although there was time enough to get back to the shop to help at closing time, my enthusiasm to find a book took me straight back home to '335 Stonehouse Lane' where I was living with my father at the time.

It was pouring with rain, and I was tempted to go back to the shop, if only to collect the errand boy's bike to ride home on. However, my head was full of thoughts, so in spite of the rain and getting John's good clothes soaking wet, I walked on.

Words kept swirling round my brain, "Confidence" "Motivation" "Copy out a book, word by word." "Say the words out loud."

I was free! I was free!

The operation had taken place.

I was not an idiot! I was somebody! I could be something. Tomorrow would not be wasted. I was in control of my own destiny. All I needed was a book and some paper, a pen and some ink and I could start!

Eventually, I reached '335'. Dad was not at home and I changed out of John's clothes and into my own dry ones and started searching the house for a book;

any book! All I wanted to do was to start copying out words.

A number of miracles had taken place, although at the time I did not see them as such:

- A lady, who had been divorced and forced to give up her nursing career, had taken a job in a grocer's shop and had discovered I was tongue-tied.

- Healthcare and an operation that had been available for years had so swiftly become appropriate to my need.

- I was overwhelmed with the sense of being free – absolutely free – with the future now in my hands.

- The new sense of confidence and high motivation to start my education: a process which in many ways was my first education and definitely critical to my future.

The sense of wonder that my treatment that day – which lasted but a few hours – and the surgical procedure itself only a few minutes – generated mixed emotions within me: anger over my lost childhood; joy that it was all over; apprehension that I had to start my education all over again but without a school structure and teachers. And the big question hanging over everything, "Would I succeed in life?"

Like many streams running into one fast-flowing river with multiple bends and twists on the way, so my

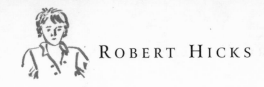

emotional elation and confusion swirled together at that time.

Little did I know that the greatest miracle in my life was about to happen! Little did I know that it would be bound up in what I now call the "Miracle Book"!

The next miracle brought with it the great discovery!

Each life is a miracle
Yet it is possible for a life merely to exist
As if it were not a miracle

Each life needs a miracle to set it free
In order for it to appreciate
That in itself it is a miracle

This freedom miracle comes about
When Jesus, the Bible and the individual
Cannot be separated

THE GREAT DISCOVERY

AV
Holy Bible
1611

THE GREAT DISCOVERY

SLUMS TO PARADISE

The next miracle that took place was in the very house of horrors that had witnessed the robbery and destruction of so much in our lives as children.

It was an evil place, where evil things happened. '335' was one of a long run of terraced houses. Built before the First World War, they were provided for farm labourers as well as the families who worked in a brick-making factory within five minutes' walk.

It was from the slums, just after the Second World War – in 1946 – that we as a family were transferred there.

This should have been paradise. Coming to this house was a real opportunity for Mom and Dad to bring up their family happily ... but that was not to be.

ALL THE BEST

Incredibly, they had everything going for them. Beside the 'Family Allowance' for six children, Dad was in employment. In total contrast to the dirty, smelly slums they had left, they now had everything such a family could wish for.

Gas had been installed and in the kitchen was a new gas cooker. Also in the kitchen was a giant cast iron boiler that once had been operated by solid fuel but had been converted to operate from gas. Each time it was lit, all of us children waited for the 'bang' while the gas pipes were cleared of air.

EVEN AN INDOOR TOILET!

Adjacent to the kitchen was a larder and – although it was cracked – there was a long marble cold slab, to help keep food fresh. Instead of an outdoor toilet shared by a multitude, we now had our own indoor toilet downstairs, with a door we could lock.

In the lounge was a black iron fireplace, recently installed, which had two additional features. One was a side stove so that the fire not only heated the room but also provided for slow cooking, and behind the fireplace were two boilers that would give at least warm water, and occasionally hot water, for the bath upstairs.

OUR OWN BATHROOM

Yes! We had a bathroom upstairs and no longer had to take down from the wall the huge tin bathtub!

Newly installed gaslights with their fragile mantles provided light in every room.

AND A GARDEN

In front of the house was a small garden and to the rear was a long garden which could have been converted to a children's play area and still have left ample room for a good vegetable patch.

Then there were neighbours who were civilised and were not always getting drunk. In my memory of the slums the drunkenness remains vivid.

FARMS AND MORE FARMS

At that time, '335' in Bartley Green village – a village mentioned in the Doomsday Book – still enjoyed numerous farms, although some were derelict. Behind us was a farm and within walking distance were others.

Incredible as it seems, I can never remember Mother or Father ever taking a walk among the fields, although we as children running wild soon discovered them.

Yet in this house that could have been a paradise home, Hell itself was created and, in my memory banks I have no recollection at all of laughter or joy or anything approximating to a family atmosphere.

BUT STILL THE SLUMS

Yes; Mom and Dad had left the slums, but tragically they had brought the worst of the slums with them.

67

And not only that, things that should never have happened to children, happened in that house. No wonder we felt robbed, abused, worthless, our only escape being when we were out in the fields, away from the house.

However, it was also inside this very house that possibly the greatest miracle took place for me.

THE SEARCH IS ON

Fuelled with ambition to find a book, the first room I went to was Jean's. She made full use of the school library and I expected to see a book there – but alas there was none. This quest made me take notice of Jean's room, perhaps for the first time. She had decorated the room in a mature adult way, making it as pretty as she could. It was a small single room, but bereft of even her few toys, including a doll. I presume they went with her when she was taken into care. I say, 'taken into care" but in actual fact she had run away from home and at this time she was living with her Aunt in the North of England, which became an unhappy experience for her. Eventually, she was sent back to the Midlands to live in an Institution.

I knew there was no point looking for a book in the boys' room. The only item in the room was the double bed that so often had accommodated five boys; three at one end and two at the other, with all our feet mingling halfway. The only benefit of five in the bed was for keeping warm in the coldest nights of winter. There was no covering on the wooden floorboards and the cold easily penetrated through the house.

I knew there was no point looking in Dad's room and in any case it was not a room I ever chose to go into.

The only thing I can ever remember Dad reading was a popular paper called the "Daily Mirror" and I suspect he could only read part of it, because later I learned from my brother John that Dad could not write and that John regularly forged Dad's signature for him on the Family Allowance book.

Something inside me was beginning to panic. I so much wanted a book and felt desperate to find one. Yet here in this house, I could find no book.

THEN THE BOOK

Then, I searched in the lounge. In the recess at the side of the fireplace was a cupboard where Dad kept his heavy army belt, which instilled fear in us all. However, I wondered if there was anything in the cupboard with words for me to copy out. It was full of rubbish of no particular value.

Eventually, I found in the corner an object, which I pulled out. It was a book with a soft covering, which later I would discover was leather. Of course, it was a

69

Bible. I did not realise that the translation was already 350 years old, full of words like 'thee' and 'thou' and other archaic expressions.

350 YEARS OLD!

The cover itself was grey and dusty, but I realised underneath it was black. I took it to the kitchen and wiped away the cobwebs and dust away. This left the cover patchy. I decided to use some black shoe polish and rub it in hard – and I have to confess that for the next few days I regretted this as the polish stained my hands!

I remember even the polish tin, because the polish had caked and so I tried to melt it on the gas stove, before transferring it in semi-liquid form onto the Bible cover.

Armed now with the Bible, I needed paper and a pen. The rest of that day I was frustrated because there was not much paper to write on and I had only a pencil. I did have an old dip-in school ink pen – a wooden stick, with a metal nib pushed on by hand. But I had no ink to dip it into.

A CAN OF INK

The next day at work, the first person that wanted to hear all my news of the Hospital was Mrs. Siddall. I explained to her not only the event of the previous day, but also the encouragement I had been given to read and write. She kindly promised to acquire some ink for me, as well as giving me some paper to get me started.

True to her word, she did, but instead of giving me a small pot of ink, she had obtained a large can of ink which I think could have filled 100 bottles – obviously she shared my enthusiasm! To write out the book I had found, which had over 1400 pages, I would need lots of paper.

WASTE PAPER

Then another small miracle took place. The "George Mason" grocer shop where I worked had been designated as a 'research' shop for one of the national research organisations called 'Neilsons' which meant that we were constantly being observed by a well-spoken gentleman who was repeatedly counting the stock to establish what we had sold. I noticed that most of his writing was done on the reverse side of used computer sheets of a large format and packed in concertina-folded reams. From time to time, one of my 'odd jobs' was to help him. I told him of my desire to write out the Bible by hand and how I did not have enough materials and I expressed a sense of envy not only at his ability to write but also the abundance of paper at his disposal.

This gentleman, who used to arrive in an old Ford

car, told me that the computer sheets were in effect 'waste paper' and he had access to an unlimited supply. He asked me how much I thought I would need. I told him 1400 sheets! He smiled, but the following day a huge quantity of these used computer sheets was given to me. Indeed, such a quantity, that it would take me several days to transfer them in sections in the basket of the delivery bike that I was allowed to use for transport home.

So now I had everything! I had a book, a pen, ink and a huge pile of used computer sheets, as well as courage and motivation.

And, with such, I set to work.

GENESIS CHAPTER ONE

I started at the first chapter of Genesis and I have to say that I found myself wasting sheet after sheet of paper because of the numerous mistakes I was making and the very large handwriting that I was using. Eventually, however, I began to form my writing smaller, trying to match the printed text on the page. Of course, I never achieved that, but slowly my writing did improve and the pages I had completed began to increase.

I remember the first time I came to the end of a complete ream of the computer sheets and the sense of great achievement I felt. Each time I filled one wad of paper, I gained fresh determination to start the next one.

FOCUSSED

Strange as it may seem, I cannot remember how long it took me to use up all the paper, or whether I was still writing two years later, or not. But what I can remember is that at Bartley Green there was no distraction from 'night life' such as there was in the City of Birmingham and I became so focussed in overcoming the years of educational neglect that I was driven by determination.

During that period that sense of commitment to what appeared to be an impossible task set in motion what has become a characteristic of my life. It has meant that during my life I have attempted things that only vision and determination and a commitment to the task would make happen.

BOTH OLD AND NEW

I am not sure when I changed and started copying out part of the New Testament at the same time as continuing with the Old Testament, but I believe it was when I had finished Exodus and realised I had a long way to go before reaching the New Testament. I then started working on two separate piles of computer sheets; one for the Old Testament and another for the New Testament. This is not the place to explain the impact that the actual words themselves were beginning to have on my life, but definitely they began to sharpen my intellect and an intelligence that had always been there now had a channel in which to express itself.

THE DIFFERENCE

As slowly my speech improved and my ability to communicate, those around me at work began to notice a difference. This included both the Manager and his Inspector.

It would be wrong for me to say that the words of the Bible had an immediate effect on me. My way into the Bible truth and eventually into the Christian faith would be a slow one. Nevertheless, the discoveries I was making and the way I was absorbing these words became part of the miracle.

MIS-SHAPEN AND WITHOUT CONTENT

For instance, I remember writing out many times those first few verses of Genesis Chapter One until such time as I was able to develop handwriting with fewer mistakes than the very earliest attempts.

I had written how God had created the heavens and earth, yet the earth had no shape and was empty. In the 350-year-old text I was using of the King James Bible, it said, "the earth was without form and void". I can remember feeling how much of my life had been "without form and void", my life was mis-shaped and without content.

As I began to read how God both shaped the earth with the mountains and the seas and the land and then filled it with living things in the seas, in the air and on the land, how I longed to be re-shaped and become full of life and beauty.

GOD'S BREATH

I remember how the Bible said that man was different to the other created things, because inside him God Himself had breathed a "living soul" into him. This left me puzzled. If God had invested so much of Himself inside man, why was it that the world had just recently been at war? Why was it that children like me had to suffer hardship, coming into this world through no choice of their own?

As I copied out the Bible, there were numerous experiences like this, when I talked to myself and reasoned within myself about what the Bible was saying and trying to relate it to human lives.

JESUS

Slowly, the word-pictures of the Bible began to materialise in my mind and the only different person amongst all the people in the Bible, as I copied it out, was Jesus. As you would expect, I had no idea of Christian theology, or of understanding what theologians call 'the Incarnation" or "the Trinity". Yet, what was very clear to me was that Jesus was advocating a new kind of living, based on love, where no one was excluded and where a relationship with God could actually happen.

It would be some years before the pages of the Bible I was copying out would be understood and appreciated. For now, I was doing what the surgeon wanted me to do. I was educating myself by reading, writing and pronouncing the words out loud as I went along.

MY 'MIRACLE BOOK'

However, a great discovery had been made: I was now in touch with my Miracle Book, and this Book would become part and parcel of my life, with a future that it would transform.

> *Human beings are different from*
> *Dogs and cats, apes and monkeys.*
>
> *Human beings need more than instinct to live,*
> *They need ways to improve morally and spiritually,*
> *Which comes from knowledge and revelation*
>
> *My 'Miracle Book' gave me such information*
> *That over a period of time changed my life.*

HUMAN SUCCESS

HUMAN SUCCESS

MOTIVATION AND CONFIDENCE

Incredibly, within a few weeks, my speech was improving dramatically and the staff at work noticed this. Within two to three months, I was beginning to hold intelligible conversations, something, which Mrs. Siddall encouraged, and something, which Mr. Hall experienced to the full. This was simply because I helped to clean up after the shop had closed and was therefore the last one to leave the shop with him.

This ability to communicate increased my desire and motivation to persevere in copying out the Bible.

GENUINE IMPROVEMENT

Although there were sections when all I saw on the page was name after name with the word "begat" repeated often, I persisted. The more I persevered, the sharper my intellect became.

I need to say here that, as a child, although I could not speak, my mind was constantly engaged and I developed powers of observation and concentration, as well as silently talking to myself and holding conversations with a host of imaginary individuals.

But now I was speaking out loud and now not in imagination, but to real people who answered me.

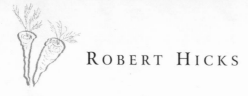
MR. WESTON

The Inspector of the shops, whom today we would call a Regional Director, was an elderly gentleman called Mr. Weston who belonged to the 'old school' who definitely believed that the customer was always right and gave each customer maximum courtesy and interest. In Mr. Weston's case, this lifetime habit of putting the customer first had its direct benefit in the way he treated his staff well too. In fact, I discovered many other Managers who were kindly to customers but just the opposite to their own staff. Mr. Weston used to commute from shop to shop by public transport. When he arrived, he was always smartly dressed in a suit and wearing a bowler hat.

MY APPRENTICESHIP

When I first started as an errand boy, although I had been told by the Careers Officer at school that if I did a good job, improved myself and showed a real interest there would be a possibility of an apprenticeship, which would give me additional education in the first few months. However, in my first year at work, Mr. Hall or Mr. Weston did not see me as a suitable candidate.

A day arrived, within a few months of the operation, when was taken into the small office at the back of the shop to see Mr. Weston on my own.

There and then he offered me an apprenticeship. What I remember about the conversation was that the course would give me real opportunities in developing skills that one day would turn me into a 'Master Grocer'. During the period of the apprenticeship, however, I would earn less because of the amount of time spent in training. Later, I learned that the Government were encouraging companies to run such schemes by contributing to the costs, and in actual fact the retail shops that participated received a good deal from the partnership as it gave them ongoing cheap labour in the process.

For me, however, becoming an Apprentice was a major step forward and I was keen to learn as much as I could.

This apprenticeship also increased my motivation to continue copying out the Bible and now I had learned to read in the process, although sadly I would never learn the art of spelling due to my dyslexia.

My aptitude for learning and progress was on fire!

AN ALL-ROUND EDUCATION

The apprenticeship offered a range of learning skills, mostly no longer needed in retailing today, but in those days of great importance. It taught me geography as I learned where the various foods came from throughout the world, as well as the history of the places where they were grown. In addition to the basic education of the course, I delved further through reading second-hand books, which I began to obtain from a place called Cotteridge not too far away where there was a huge shop that, true to its name, was called "Treasure Trove". The numerous treasures I obtained there started my love of books.

Of course, with geography, I began to learn world history. As I began to learn world history, I also became interested in the types of books that formed the basis of history. Somewhere in my mid- to late-teens, I began to read the Greek Philosophers and what was known as the 'golden period of Greek history'. I found the dialogue approach in Philosophy in the way Plato highlighted the brilliance of Socrates, to my liking. Maybe those years of observation and talking to myself with imaginary people, had established a way of thinking that made it easier for me to follow philosophy.

So geography and history had expanded into philosophy and as I copied out the Bible I also gained theology. All this was impacting on my work as a Grocer.

No longer was I an Errand Boy, but now an Assistant Provision Hand. Then I became the Manager of a counter as well as going away to schools for additional training. Before long, I knew how to bone

and cut up an entire pig, as well as how to skin a whole range of cheeses and to cut them by hand to weight precisely into chunks of four ounces, eight ounces, twelve ounces and sixteen ounces, according to customers' requirements.

Beside practical work, such as cutting 'ham on the bone', weighing and packing sugar and butter (with no refrigeration!) there was also training in wholesale buying and selling, warehousing, distribution, handling money and book-keeping, as well as the joy of using artistic talent in displaying goods in the window. Using cans of beans to create a gravity-defying pyramid was a science in itself! For my window displays, I won many first, second and third prizes!

In those days, I learned skills in retailing which reached back over 200 years, and yet in my own time would disappear as we entered into the 'supermarket' and 'pre-packed food' world.

RELIEF MANAGER

Before I completed my apprenticeship, Mr. Weston came to me and said he wanted me to be a Relief Manager that very day as a Manager had become ill at another shop. I was only 18 at the time, and could not believe the transformation that had taken place since my 15th birthday, when I had fought physically with my Dad to bring an end to his dominant bullying tactics, which in many cases were violent. Yet, within three years, and two-and-a-half years since my operation, I was now a Relief Manager of a shop.

Those years in marketing are left for my second book, "A Boy Speaks". For now, all I can say is that, during the following three years, I managed numerous shops and was so successful that Mr. Weston told me I was the most successful Relief Manager in "George Masons" and he preferred to keep me as his Relief Manager, than to promote me to Manage my own shop.

Although I was pleased to hear of the confidence he had in me, I was disappointed that I was not to become Manager of my own shop.

TIN HUT CHURCH

During these years, I was becoming aware of the Bible talking about how Christians met together as a church, with various cities being mentioned by name. Something inside me told me that I ought to be attending church. I started attending a small church that I could walk to in about ten or fifteen minutes from home.

This was an independent church where only a few folk met together. It was really a mission for children's work and not much beside. They met in a simple hall constructed of corrugated metal. It definitely looked more like a tin-hut than a 'church'. Around a dozen people were active in the church, although in the Sunday School there would be 50-60 children.

Considering that I had no church background, I think they were surprised at how much I knew about the Bible when I was among them. Mid-week, they had a meeting for Prayer and Bible Study, which I found myself attending and asking questions way beyond my years.

MR. BARNWELL

One of the leaders in the church, Mr. Barnwell, at the end of a service asked me a direct question, "Are you born again? Have you received Jesus Christ as your Saviour?"

My answer was in the negative. I had, by this time, read and copied out the third chapter of John's Gospel but the concept of being "born again" was only a fraction of what I had written out and had not appeared to me of great drama. However, I could see that Mr. Barnwell was keen that I should experience being "born again" and he said all I needed do was to offer a genuine but simple prayer telling Jesus I was sorry for my sins and inviting Him into my life as my Saviour, and then God would do the rest.

Part of what he said rang true to me. So, when he invited me to say a prayer with him, I did so. I think at the time I felt this was more for his benefit than mine.

As a result of this five-minute conversation and prayer, the members of the church saw me as part of the church family and I was treated as one of their own thereafter.

There were many human benefits that came my way in the little church. I was invited to various homes for tea, as well as Sunday lunch. This introduced me to the caring, loving side of humanity, which had been in very short supply in my life up to that time.

MR. WISE

Mr. Wise was a bread deliveryman who sold his greenhouse and, out of the proceeds of the sale, gave me ten shillings, which in today's currency would be £0.50 ($0.30), but in those days was a sum of much greater value and a generous gift. The purpose was for me to acquire a shirt, trousers and a pair of shoes, all of which I desperately needed. That generous gift from Mr. Wise with the love that was behind it, influenced my attitude to money and wealth more than any other single event that has taken place in my life.

BIBLE PREACHING

Also, by hearing the Bible preached in church, my motivation was fuelled to complete copying out the Bible and, in so doing, I increased my appreciation of it.

JOHN CHAPTER THREE VERSE SIXTEEN

Then, one night, I had what can only be described as "my Damascus experience". I was alone in the house, my siblings scattered and only Dad living at home with me – if 'living' is the word.   It was way past midnight and with the various new-found experiences at work and at church, for some reason I felt very much alone, isolated and with a mammoth mountain still in front of me to climb. I needed help – but most of all, I needed love.

The gas needed money in the meter, so the lights had long gone out. As a double-decker bus made its journey past the house up to the terminus at Jiggins Lane, light and shadow danced around the ceiling through the uncurtained window.

I found myself crying; not heavy sobs, but tears beginning to flow. Some of the words of Mr. Barnwell were ringing in my ears. Definitely, I had never felt myself to be a sinner. I felt more sinned against, than a sinner.   But I had felt unloved and unwanted for so long in my life.

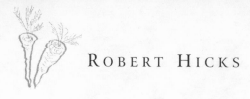

Slowly, I slid out of the bed and, kneeling beside that old bed which I had shared so often with my four brothers, I began to say a prayer. I called upon God and I called upon Jesus to come into my life and to forgive whatever needed to be forgiven and to make me aware of their love for me personally. The text of John chapter 3 verse 16 kept coming into my prayers and my heart wanted so much for it to be true.

How long I was kneeling and praying, I don't know. But it must have been quite a time because a second bus shone the beams of its light across the room and pulled me out of my praying and I realised I was thoroughly cold and my knees were stiff and I needed to get the blood circulating again before I got back into bed.

MY 'MIRACLE BOOK'

I wish, readers, I could say that, from that moment I was aware of the love of God and the presence of Jesus in my life. But, what I can say is that from that moment, slowly, very slowly, I became aware of a dimension of a living God and an ever available Jesus in a spiritual sense and from that moment, the Bible became a Miracle Book in my own soul in a way that it had not done before.

The Bible I had been copying out, as I have already mentioned, was the King James Version that then was

350 years old. Maybe it would have been wiser for me to have had a modern translation. Maybe, then, I would have understood more quickly what the Bible was saying. However, that old translation had a poetical feel and a rhythm about it that was much easier to retain in the mind. I have now discovered that most modern translations still have a long way to go before they reach the beauty of the language that the King James Bible gave to me.

MANAGER AT 21

Following that experience, my confidence grew even stronger and, by the age of 21, I was a Manager of the very same shop in Selly Oak where I had started as an Errand Boy.

It was intended, however, that they would keep that shop open only a few months, because "George Mason" had a second shop not too far down the road in Bournbrook. Once that shop was completed, they were going to transfer the business from Selly Oak to Bournbrook.

However, the moment I became Manager, I was determined that they would not close my shop down! Through hard work and some unexpected opportunities, I increased the turnover by 300%, which guaranteed the shop continuing to trade for another 20 years! It also gave me opportunities of

promotion as a Manager for the future, where the retail revolution was taking place.

'TESCO'

Before long, I found myself working for a new retailer who was putting fear into the old established businesses throughout the country. It was called 'TESCO'. I started with 'TESCO' as a Manager, then as a Regional Director. During this period, I began to realise the negative side of the retail revolution and I was pleased when the opportunity came my way to be the Marketing Director of what was then a huge retail operation, the 'Co-Operative Society'.

'CO-OP'

So I became responsible for the 'Birkenhead & District Co-Operative Society' and in their employment I was selected to open up the first 'out-of-town' hypermarket called the "Woodchurch Superstore". In recent years, the site has been obtained by 'ASDA'.

It was after completing the "Woodchurch Superstore" and receiving recognition nationally for my contribution to retailing, that my love for the Holy Bible and books influenced me in making a career move that, on paper, appeared impossible.

I became a publisher.

PUBLISHER

The movement known as the "Scripture Union" which operated from London, desperately needed help as it was losing in its publishing division £1000 a week, and this was putting a huge strain on its missionary work. Mr. Robert Horne, who at that time was the Chairman & Chief Executive of 'Horne Brothers' the clothing retail company, interviewed me.

Before long, a move from the Wirral to London took place and for the next six years, I worked with Scripture Union, developing a new range of publishing programmes.

The first full year resulted not in a loss, but in a profit that could be invested in new publishing programmes; a profit greater than the total turnover of the previous year. I was to receive many shocks in publishing, and made many mistakes in the process of learning, but I am so grateful for my six years in Scripture Union, following which I set up my own Company and, since those days, have been involved in both secular and Christian publishing in many parts of the world.

As the title of this chapter indicates, my careers would be seen as a 'human success'.

REAL SUCCESS

My reason for heading the chapter in this way is because I wish to acknowledge that the 'human' success was a by-product of the miracle that took place when I started copying out the Bible as a boy of 15.

The real success was not that human by-product, but the way the Holy Bible had liberated me inside my soul. It had set free from my childhood, it had educated me, it had given me ethical principles that were worth trying to follow, and it had brought me into a Kingdom that Jesus described as the "Kingdom of Heaven". Belonging to that Kingdom, and becoming a disciple and follower of Jesus Christ was the real success story.

Although I do thank God for the 'human success', it fades into insignificance compared to the true success of making contact with the real God and appreciating Jesus Christ as both Saviour and Lord, the Light of the World, a companion through all the challenges of life. Definitely, the greatest challenge for me was when my wife Joyce was diagnosed with terminal cancer and given only six months to live.

How would the 'Miracle Book' continue to play its part, when suddenly and unexpectedly I had to face the shadow of death and a dark future?

JOHN CHAPTER THREE VERSE SIXTEEN

"For God
So loved
The world (including me)
That He gave
His only Son
That whoever believes (including me)
In Him
Shall not perish (will not be wasted
in this life, or the next)
But have
Everlasting life."

The way this world-famous part of the Bible grew on me, made me aware I was not alone. The purpose of my life was not to be shapeless and empty. It was not to be a waste. Rather, besides embracing God's love in the supreme love of Jesus on the cross, I also would be the recipient of the very best of God Himself – Everlasting life! A life changing thought, if ever there was one.

John's Gospel refers to God as Father over 100 times. Now that's a life-changing thought!

MARRIAGE, FAMILY
AND BEREAVEMENT

MARRIAGE, FAMILY AND BEREAVEMENT

MANAGEMENT AND MARRIAGE

I was married at the same time that I became a Manager of my own shop, even though initially I was only to be a 'caretaker' Manager until the shop closed. I was 21 at that time.

I had left home before my 17th birthday and lodged with various Christian couples until I was married.

Each time I did Relief Managing, I was able to share the additional money I earned with those whose needs were greater than mine. What motivated me to do this, I have recorded in "A Boy Speaks".

THE AINSLIE FAMILY

One of the families who included me in their home life was the Ainslie family. The father, Mr. Will Ainslie, had himself had a difficult childhood and home background and had left home early. He had received little education as a child, but he had a disciplined mind and had taught himself. When I came into his family life, he was a Senior Lecturer at Birmingham University. Tragically, he died young. One of the great honours of my life was when his widow Jessie, over thirty years later, requested that I should conduct her

funeral service. It was a joy to be able to speak of the devoted husband and wife, now reunited in heaven, even though their arrivals there were separated by so many years.

Even now, I can picture the entire Ainslie family in those early days. I gladly acknowledge the many benefits I received from that family in my late teens and early twenties, and the friendship I was able to maintain with Mrs. Ainslie through the years.

SCOTLAND

One of those happy occasions was when the Ainslie family invited me to share in a family holiday on one of the small islands of Scotland at a place called Millport, Firth of Clyde. At the Christian Guest House where we stayed, I met my future wife Joyce - a young attractive intelligent and keen Christian. Amazingly, she had fallen in love with me; a love which never diminished in spite of the many flaws in my makeup and my constant fight with the negative side of my father's influence.

ANDREW, PETER, JULIA AND JOANNA

Over the next few years, we welcomed the arrival of four children; two boys, Andrew and Peter, then two girls, Julia and Joanna. There was also one child lost between the boys. Alongside my successes in retailing

and publishing, there was always Joyce and the family.

JULIA'S MARRIAGE

In the fullness of time, our elder daughter Julia
announced her engagement to a lovely and sensitive
young man called Paul. Twelve weeks after their
wedding and in the year of our own Silver Wedding
Anniversary, Joyce was diagnosed with cancer. I was
told, in the opinion of the surgeon, to expect the worst
within six months. Following the death of my wife, I
wrote "An Appreciation" which is now included, in the
way I originally wrote it.

I also wrote for Joyce, and with Joyce, paraphrases
of Psalms and other parts of the Bible, especially one
on the resurrected body, which became very important
to Joyce.

MY APPRECIATION

Over 25,000 of the booklet "Joyce – An Appreciation"
were eventually produced and many found their way
into the Hospices throughout the United Kingdom
and I hope that by including the text here, it may
continue to be of help to some, especially those going
through difficult times or facing what is common to us
all: human weakness and the closing of this earthly
life.

JOYCE

THIS IS OUR STORY

*An inspiration for all who are facing
death or bereavement*

JOYCE

ROMANCE TO APPRECIATION

Romance was what started it all, when in Scotland, I met this seventeen year old girl, full of life, attractive, with soft blue eyes. She was wearing a yellow dress which has remained my favourite colour ever since.

Responsibility was soon blended with romance, as we married the following year, and were blessed with four children over the next seven years.

Full of constant change were these hectic 'responsible' years, which Joyce was more than capable of. There is no doubt that Joyce lived life to the full, giving herself to her husband, growing family, friends near and far, as well as welcoming strangers.

She always encouraged her husband in his enthusiasm to accept new challenges, which meant moving seven times making new homes all over England.

Once the children became more independent in their later years and early twenties, for the first time a difficult period emerged as both of us were re-evaluating our roles, both together and separately for the future. This was, as for many, a difficult time, but it was not long before it gave way to a most rewarding stage of our marriage, which can only be summed up in one word 'appreciation'.

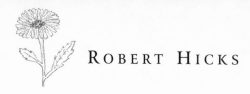
Romance to appreciation, was the way we both described our relationship when coming up to our eldest daughter's wedding in the same month as our silver wedding anniversary in September.

Romance... to appreciate each other, what a prospect for us both to move forward to this important stage of our marriage.

Joyce's final words on an amateur video at the wedding were, "We would do it all over again, what fun".

What fun! Within twelve weeks we would begin a two and a half year journey that would test to the full our romance to appreciation in life as well as our faith in the love of God.

Now was the winter.

ONE DAY IN JANUARY

We had faced twenty four January's together, and this our twenty fifth, was similar to many others in that it was wet and cold but by mid afternoon it would be a day we would never forget, for it would leave its mark upon us for the rest of our lives.

My beautiful wife, Joyce, had cancer, melanoma, a fast growing cancer, rare in England but wide spread in the hot climates of Australia and California.

Lethal was the word the surgeon used; I remember looking into his experienced face, for he was past

retirement and only working part time. How many times, I thought, had he broken the news to many couples, like he was breaking this to us? News that would be so shattering.

"Is it curable?", was my first response. Joyce sitting numbed quietly just listening. "No, I am sorry it has spread to the lymph system, there is very little we can do."

"Is it terminal?" I asked. "Not yet, but you need to know that it is unpredictable and lethal".

"Is it controllable?" was my third question. "Again we can only try" was his answer. "But we will do all we can" he promised.

"How long do we have?" was my response, "Melanoma is usually a fast spreading cancer, but it is unpredictable, we have no way of knowing".

I remember my mind being crystal clear, trying to obtain maximum information at this first consult-ation, but in it all I knew deep down that we had been given dynamite, alight, and not knowing how long the fuse was.

Two tumours were removed within days, and during that time we discovered in the medical records that Joyce had a mole removed some seventeen years earlier that had been malignant. This meant that we had been spared all these years to bring up the four children we had been blessed with, as well as to

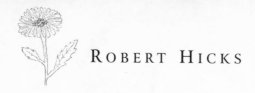
accomplish so much together.

From that cold wet day in January our lives had been violently interrupted and nothing would be the same again.

FIRST STEPS

In the early days of hearing the news we were in shock, nothing in the world at large or in our own personal lives, seemed important any more.

Breaking the news to the children and Joyce's parents was not going to be easy. Simple everyday things, like going shopping, were now a burden. The normal small talk in conversation with family and friends had become a strain.

We knew we had to face the fact that Joyce was now living under a death sentence, and we didn't know when it would come, but we knew it was only a matter of time. Time, even that now seemed warped.

Because Joyce had seen me as the person with imagination and ideas, as well as being unafraid of any challenge, she believed in those early days that if any one could find a cure it was me! I was devastated by her faith in me, feeling totally paralysed to help her in the way she wanted. Deep down I know I was also proud and humbled by this kind of faith. But this was on challenge in human terms I knew I could not win.

We agreed to divide our energies; Joyce would

investigate alternative or complimentary medicine, while I would concentrate on the constructive orthodox approach.

All the information I received was painful. Two surgeons, two specialists in cancer, four doctors, all gave the same verdict, which was "It's only a matter of time". One of my friends was a doctor who I respected, I told him the news, pretending it was somebody else in trouble, so that I would obtain an objective evaluation. He also gave Joyce a short time.

They all said the same sad news, that if the cancer attacks the vital organs, which is what they expected, then it would only be a few months. They also offered the hope that sometimes there is a remission, but this was unusual and only lasted for a time.

Joyce collapsed and was rushed into hospital, her liver was infected, they feared the worse, and we all thought we were going to lose Joyce immediately. In actual fact it was hepatitis, which meant that Joyce was home again within two to three weeks. The fact that her liver was weakened made me even more convinced that we didn't have much time before the cancer took over.

The investigation into alternative medicine came up with a fifty year old treatment called Gerson Therapy. This was the most demanding of therapies involving thirteen organic juices a day pressed by special machinery. In addition to this she would have to have four enemas a day, injections. Take ghastly castor oil as well as calves liver every day after they had been converted into juice.

Joyce committed herself to the diet with the quiet strength and courage only she was capable of. So far no hope, but the claims of the Gerson diet gave Joyce something practical to do.

Because it would take time to obtain the equipment and organise everything we decided to take an instant 'off the peg' holiday and found ourselves, twenty-four hours later, in Tenerife.

MORE THAN COPING

We had a self catering apartment, totally secluded, so we spent this precious week, reading, talking, praying, loving, and more loving, by allowing an excessive appreciation of each other in every way possible. It was the best holiday of our lives, if only we had approached our other holidays with this commitment to each other.

So far I have mentioned what was on offer in the medical world, but we had also talked of what we could experience in terms of Christian healing. Being Christians we had, as you would expect, sort help in Christian healing. A recognised gifted Christian from a local church came and prayed for Joyce's healing.

Joyce witnessed to the fact that she had "been healed in her spirit", and all fear had been removed and she knew from that day that she was safe in hands stronger than her own, the medical people, the Gerson therapy, and her husband's, family and friends.

They had prayed for healing of the body. Joyce believed she had been given something greater. A short time later we had at the same church, a time of confession, prayer and the anointing of oil. Joyce now believed that she had embraced the grace of God concerning healing and felt confident in His sovereignty. "Thy will be done", did not become "This is your will". She was at peace and that peace was never going to leave her.

After our 'best' holiday, we settled down to this demanding diet. We had now embraced what in effect was a self inflicting prison within our own home, but what was important was that we were facing the reality of the situation. We were not putting our heads in the sand or running away.

By facing this cancer, we soon realised that many other people were suffering like we were. They needed help, and Joyce was going to play her part. We had an apartment for our publishing friends that was used in connection with our work. Joyce took this over and soon three other cancer sufferers were there. Joyce knew that what had happened to her had enabled her to sympathise and help other people. We saw two of these three people pass away. The first said the last months in the apartment was the best time during her long sickness. She had cancer of the bone, which is very painful. Before the second lady died she also expressed similar sentiments.

In spite of the demanding diet, Joyce organised a conference week at home to which over fifty people came. A young beautiful lady, just turned twenty-two came, she had been given two years to live. When I looked at her radiant personality something inside told me that she had the mark of heaven upon her and she would not last out the two years. In a sensitive way I told this to her mother and explained my conviction. They also started the diet programme, which they kept up for fourteen months, but on a plane to Mexico this lovely girl died and went to heaven.

Because I did not have the same conviction in the diet as my dear wife, I continued to select passages and promises from the Bible and paraphrasing them as well as reading them to Joyce. This was something I had started when Joyce was in hospital in the early days. These eventually became two books, 'Healing Words' which I did *with* Joyce and 'A Taste of Heaven' which I did *for* Joyce.

During this time, well-meaning Christian friends were promising Joyce healing by the authority of Jesus

over the power of Satan, which they believed was the cause of Joyce's cancer. Joyce knew in her heart, and from the promises in the Scriptures this was not the case. She was in God's hands and being there she believed that in His love, His sovereignty would decide the outcome.

We were not only coping, but also beginning to live a rich, full life, being involved with the lives of many other people. Perplexed yes, but also honoured.

WHAT ARE FRIENDS FOR?

Joyce had received hope and encouragement in her spirit, faith in her convictions, love in her emotions, which expressed themselves in seeking to help others. She also would need help from her friends, and suddenly we both would discover who our friends really were. Beside the helpers, who were paid for, Marina, a lovely Christian lady and our eldest daughter's mother in law, came to help.

If ever there was an angel with large wings that embraced, it was Marina. She committed herself to three half days every week for the full eighteen months of this diet. This would be a demanding commitment but she entered into it with such a refreshing attitude that all of us felt helped, especially Joyce. In human terms we do not know what we would have done without her.

During this time our two daughters gave birth, first to a girl and then to our second daughter a son, Amy and Sam. Again, in this we witnessed something remarkable.

First Joyce had embraced the prayer in the Psalms that God would let her see her children's children, this was at a time that it seemed most unlikely, and although this was not fulfilled totally as no doubt more children will come, she rejoiced in seeing her first two grandchildren.

But to me an even greater miracle had taken place, which was, that Joyce was never bitter, jealous, or envious that Marina would have the greater blessing of seeing our first granddaughter grow up. Marina herself found this humbling, but when God heals the spirit it is a wonderful thing to witness, and Joyce was healed in her spirit.

Other friends came to help, some simply by sending flowers, especially when Joyce was spending one of her frequent stays in hospital, others by coming round to talk and to keep us company. But the friends, who we thought would be there to help, never came. How true it is that a friend in need is a friend indeed.

One of our close friends of many years standing, who had moved not too far away from us was noticed by her absence. Joyce on one occasion saw her shopping locally, and for a long time was troubled by

this lack of sensitivity, love and care. We both had a lot to learn, which was that many people do not know how to handle serious sicknesses and dying. Their staying away was a reflection of their own fears. If only someone could help them to overcome this understandable fear. Alas they never knew the joy of being part of the day-to-day encouragement of Joyce, but Joyce, by understanding their fears, gained peace even in this. Other friends from a distance started prayer groups, others by constantly remembering us in their prayer time, both personally and in their local church.

Christians from different denominations and cultural experiences were praying for us. Our friends from the Bible Society were also now beginning to hold us up in prayer. Practical friendship, close friendship, friendship by flowers, cards, letter, prayer meetings all helped. Indeed we discovered for ourselves the experience that Paul entered into when in prison when he said to his friends that had been supporting him, that their prayers had 'made the difference'. It puts their prayer on the same level as the ever loving flow of Christ's Spirit into His own life.

We in our extreme situation, with eight operations and nearly forty tumours removed as well as the demanding diet, felt the comfort and love of friends. How privileged we were, how precious.

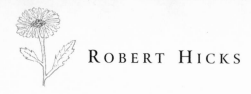

FACING ILLNESS

Because of the kind of melanoma Joyce had, she was in constant pain, and because of the demands of the diet program, she was not allowed to take painkillers or even aspirins.

The first major surgery was on the right hand side of her beautiful face, she always had a dimple there, one of my favourite kissing places, but when the tumour threatened to burst the skin as well as to spread to her eyes, nose and her lips we decided the time had come for it to be removed. The surgeon thought that beside plastic surgery she might have to have a skin graft. Fortunately he was able to avoid this.

This was the first of many operations, eight in all, with nearly forty tumours removed and lots of pain and suffering. How did Joyce handle this? She believed that God's grace was always with her. She knew that friends were with her in many ways. She became involved in the lives of others, but now she started dried flower arranging to raise money to support other cancer friends.

After two or three months work we held two special days at home where over two hundred flower arrangements were sold. These would be a permanent reminder in friends' homes of the faith, love and courage of Joyce.

Was all this a distraction to the cancer? Maybe,

but more important it was an involvement in the lives of others. All of our life together had been shared, our home, our time, our talents, now our suffering. Somehow Joyce knew that this experience of pain and sickness was something that could be turned into a benefit to others.

She was not going to shut herself away with her own grief and expect others to pick up the pieces. She would take the initiative in every way possible. She was not going to be a burden to anyone, she was going to receive help and also give help. This was her way of facing her illness.

Because she was increasingly being weakened by the many operations and the spread of tumours all over her body, she obviously needed more rest, but even this she would turn into a blessing. Many hours a day we would cuddle up to each other on the bed or settee, with a blanket over us and just love each other. Sexual relationship was becoming a thing of the past, yet physical contact, emotional peace and spiritual awareness, all underneath the umbrella of love was growing and growing.

She received great strength from these times in my arms and although initially the dominant element in me was caring, I knew something spectacular was happening to me, I could only call this a 'therapeutic sensation'. Slowly I was falling in love with Joyce as if

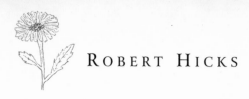

she was that sweet seventeen-year-old girl, in that yellow dress she was wearing nearly thirty years ago. I eventually became madly in love again.

To fall in love this way twice, with the same woman, is something I cannot describe in words. From the beginning to the end and everything in between, all that I received from Joyce made me realise that I was a privileged person

All this was a way of facing illness. It meant accepting, discovering, growing and experiencing It meant submitting to the pain and from that pain entering into a whole new reality of life, by reaching out to others.

THE FAMILY

Each of the four children, Andrew; twenty five, Peter; twenty two, Julia; twenty one, and Joanna who was nineteen, found it difficult that their always dependable mother, who was always available to them, might soon be taken away from them.   They wept with me as I told them the news. Each of them would respond to the devastating news in their own way and it would be insensitive of me to recall their feelings and reactions.

What I can share with you however, is the way Joyce responded to their needs. We have always been a close family and because of Joyce's generosity of

spirit, she enabled us to share our fullness with others. It is no surprise that after a time our four children began to trust her optimism, they began to rely on her in the same way as they always had. Because of who their mother was, they naturally accepted that she would be involved with other people as well.

Julia was married, about to move near us, the other three were still at home. Because I did not want them to see the gradual effect of the cancer on their energetic mother I encouraged them to find their own apartments, which they did. This turned out to be a wise decision. Joyce received great joy from her children and support. She also made allowances for the effect the cancer would have upon them.

Beside the children there was Joyce's parents, now in their mid seventies. Over the years they had spent many months each year with us, especially holiday times. Just a year earlier we had taken them to Cyprus for their golden wedding anniversary. They were very precious to Joyce, being their only daughter, and she was concerned how they would take it, but she also knew that they had to be told. Both could not believe the news when they heard it, and they were obviously distraught.

But even here something wonderful took place. Joyce's mother received new energy, she became a younger person, and any way in which they both could

help they did so. Joyce's optimism also affected grandma. Grandfather like myself, was pessimistic about the diet and the cancer, but again, like me, kept it to himself.

Joyce had one elder brother, and although they had been kept apart by distance, it was obvious that between them was a very close affection and Joyce felt this pain as well as the pain of the cancer. It is true that when part of the family suffer all the family suffer. It is also true that Joyce had to bear the pain of seeing her own children and parents in pain, as well as having to fight against the pain that the cancer was giving her physically.

The family had, and was experiencing, a whole new range of emotions that had both negative and positive effects. Inevitably this would bring to Joyce and I both benefits and problems. Consequently it became a time of new understanding facing this new situation, and we also needed God's grace each time a problem occurred, which came as a direct result of the cancer.

Joyce and I were going to need not only grace in fighting cancer and facing death, but also for all the additional pressures that were coming our way and affecting the family.

J O Y C E

SPIRITUAL DIMENSION

There are many people who have a dominance in their lives of one kind or another. A close friend is a physical enthusiast, going in for demanding physical competitions. Others are predominantly intellectual while others have a high dose of emotionalism, but I had only ever read of people with a spiritual dominance until death, our unwelcome guest, appeared.

Joyce always was a spiritual person, with part of her spirit wanting eagle's wings to fly away, but her unassuming practical, no nonsense personality was what we had witnessed over the years. But this caterpillar had become a butterfly; she was undergoing a transformation before us. This potential was always there, her faith, her acceptance of God, Jesus and spiritual experience was always part of her life, but this was something else. As already mentioned, she did not hide herself from reality but she did make time, and to her important time, to be alone with herself so that she could receive God's love and truth.

In addition to this she had a few friends with whom she could talk to about her spiritual quest, as well as myself. All this contributed to the development of her own spiritual life. She first had to find herself. Up until now she had generously given herself to her husband, children and others, and in that order. Now she needed time to discover what made her her - that

discovery she made in a remarkably short time. She loved and appreciated who she was, and what God's love had given her in life.

But something else was happening; she began not only to believe the actual promises, but started experiencing them as well. How was this achieved? First, by developing an attitude that refused to condemn anyone or anything that had within it reflections of God. Every person was important and had something to contribute. Any good from any source, to her was good. Also at this time she was developing an incredible ability of imagination, meditation and prayer.

She began to move into the picture language of the Bible. The Lord was her Shepherd; she could in her imagination walk with Him in pastures green. The Garden of God with rivers of living water was an actual place that she could go to and be refreshed in her spirit by His goodness. Her mind was opened in a way that I had never witnessed before. The Psalms in particular gave her great encouragement and hope.

Slowly she made the psalms that she would meditate on, somehow speak to her, as a result of this I would take the psalms she selected and turn them into inspirational readings that would appeal to her own situation. All this was meat to her soul and air to her lungs. God's word was working for her.

JOYCE

Our time together was becoming richer and richer, but for me it was partially an exercise of the mind and the will, for Joyce it was like growing wings for her spirit.

We published a range of small books on 'Why Fear'; 'Why Cry'; 'Why Give Up'; and 'Why Worry'. Also a range of small books on love and heaven, but something of Joyce was now getting through to me so I found myself condensing and re-writing the book of Revelation, which eventually came out under the title of 'A Taste of Heaven'. To Joyce, however, it was not a taste but heaven itself.

Prayer, meditation, faith in God's promises, became the means by which she rose to heights and experiences of which I was and still am a stranger. Can God's love and truth have such an effect on a single quiet human being? Joyce is a testimony that says yes, not once but a thousand times.

This process would go on for two and a half years, and eventually when she faced the last remnants of death itself, they would be her wings that would take her into the other world.

This living in God's word by prayer, meditation and imagination reflected itself by her desire to help those who were less fortunate than ourselves. For her it worked, and worked powerfully.

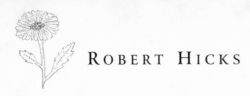

FACING DEATH ITSELF

The last enemy of us all is death. We all must die, but few of us are prepared. If Joyce had died when rushed into hospital the first time, she was still prepared, but to live in her presence over two and a half years in which she fought cancer and grew spiritually, was both a painful but also rewarding experience.

Right from the start she was not afraid, she was absolutely convinced that God knew what he was doing, and she saw clearly that the words of Jesus concerning the rain as well as the sun falling on the righteous and unrighteous sensible and logical. She had that kind of faith.

It is true that she was optimistic about the diet program, but when she counted thirty tumours growing some way into the diet, she accepted the possible and inevitable outcome. Because the tumours had not, as expected, attacked her vital organs she wondered whether the diet was keeping them away, and if so, all its demands were worth it. Unfortunately, it was only after her last operation that the surgeon concluded that she had an unusual form of melanoma that affected the fatty tissues beneath the skin, and not her vital organs. So we did not really need to go through the demanding diet programme.

But now death was upon us, and what lessons were there to learn from looking it in the face. In the last

JOYCE

two weeks of Joyce's life I noticed the wild poppies in our garden. The more the sun's rays and warmth hit the petals, the more they opened up and the wider they opened the weaker they became at the roots of the petals. So when a gentle breeze came, the green grass would be covered with petals.

So it was with Joyce. She had opened up to the warmth of God's love and the rays of heaven and was being disconnected from time, her environment, home, and all things relating to our lives. We had already agreed that death was like going to sleep on a cold October day to be awakened in the warmth and vitality of a day in mid spring.

My darling of nearly thirty years was going to sleep soon to wake up in a new, cleaner, better place far away from all the pain and suffering. She was going to receive the reward for her faith and love, which was salvation in all its completeness.

A week before she died we had our last long talk together in the early hours of the morning. We talked of everything and nothing, we renewed for the thousandth time our love for each other, and she again encouraged me to find a new wife with a loving and kind disposition, not a person caught up with materialistic things. She entrusted to me, yet again, her parents and our children and their children.

We had so much and yet nothing to seek in terms

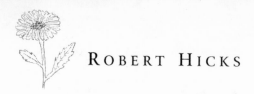

of forgiveness from each other, we were as one, as only two weak human beings could possibly be. I could not hold her for she now had too many tumours to count all over her skin, so we held hands and kissed and kissed again and again. This time was the most important and precious time of the two and a half years we had together.

I had always feared that when the time came to face this final stage I would stand naked before her, for all the things I should have done and all the things I had done that I knew had hurt her, but it was not like that, for in this act, this moment we both were pure to each other.

Death had made us appreciate each other, death had brought with it a vitality of a kind that we had not experienced before in our lives, now death for Joyce was a new adventure, which she was ready to take. Facing death together made us both realise over a long period of time that it is not what we have, or even what we have accomplished, or what any particular types of talents or gifts we may possess that matters, but rather who we are by God's grace.

So the unwelcome guest had come, Joyce reached out and took him by the hand and left her loving family in God's strong hands as she continued her courageous adventure into a territory that in her spirit she had already possessed.

JOYCE

WHAT NOW?

So we have to face the future without the best of mothers and the closest of wives. Instead of a funeral we had a thanksgiving. Joyce had requested no mourning clothes and no flowers but the gifts to the local hospice. Over two hundred people from far and near were drawn to this day.

Ten friends who loved Joyce, covering the past twenty-eight years, gave testimony to her faith, hope, love, courage and generosity of spirit. By praising this quiet yet exceptional person who had given herself to her husband, children, friends and strangers, they were praising all women with the same attitude, that are seldom recognised in our age of plastic heroes.

But, now grief, fear, anger, loneliness and a sense of being cheated, by myself and all the family. We had been given a great gift bound up in one wonderful human being and it seemed that as if before we had time to fully appreciate and enjoy her, she had been taken away from us.

The following day after the thanksgiving, we scattered the ashes and the twenty-seven yellow roses, one for each of our married years, in a fast flowing stream. We also cast a wreath from the mother of the young beautiful girl who died on the aeroplane, for we knew that Joyce would be now rejoicing with her in heaven.

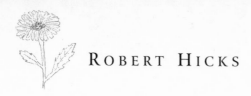

Still as I looked and saw the yellow dots vanish down the river I wondered, what now? The children will have to learn without the dependable mother, they no longer have the benefit of her practical love and transparent faith. Now they will have to learn for themselves the richness of those qualities that she had in abundance.

My life also was having to undergo a radical change, for we had done everything together and my dependency on her, as I had come to realise over the last few years was complete. Now I was alone.

I prayed that God would let me have one small glimpse of her in heaven, glowing, but the same faith she had developed was all that was on offer. God's grace and my faith was the combination. She taught me that love was real. She loved me, how she loved me, if one could love another like that, then how great is God's love.

She taught me life was full. All my tomorrows had a wealth, a meaning, an adventure and excitement. She understood that it was unlikely that I would be able to live without a companion, only time will tell, but in her love, she only wanted what was good for me.

Our home was now empty, my life was also empty, both inside and outside was void. But she taught me that God's grace would fill this space. I was not alone, even when all my senses told me I was alone. She gave me so much that on the day she died, I knew that she had departed from a weak and damaged body and had moved immediately into the presence of Jesus. So what now? If Joyce could look into darkness of death and see the light and love of God, so I can look into the darkness of tomorrow and seek that same light and love of God.

On the day my darling wife faced the final moment of death I wrote the following poem, a reflection of my love for her.

"Now
My kisses
Become red tears
Falling
On fertile ground
So yellow petals
Will dress my princess
For eternity"

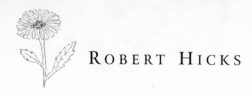

ROBERT HICKS

A selection of Robert's reflections on Psalms and 1 Corinthians 15, read to Joyce following her many operations in hospital.

Growing strong again

> *Lord, I want to be like the trees that grow strong,*
> *Beside the running stream,*
> *To see my children's children*
> *And still not be sick or tired:*
> *To see all that I do has meaning and direction.*
> *Lord I know that happiness*
> *Is finding joy in you and what you say.*
> *This happiness I seek in the daytime and at night.*
> ***From Psalm 1***

I can trust

> *My Lord*
> *I can trust what you say*
> *Each promise from you*
> *Is as genuine as silver,*
> *Even silver that has been*
> *Refined seven times*
> *In the hottest of fires.*
> *Yes I do trust what you say.*
> ***From Psalm 12***

Safe in the times of darkness

My God is all I need
He is my protection
I am safe with Him
He protects me like a shield
He defends me from attack
He keeps me safe.
In times of darkness
He is my light,
Even the darkness of my mind.
What God has done
What God has said
Can be depended upon
By everyone who seeks Him.
He is my God
Who makes me strong.
All my tomorrows are
Safe with my God.
From Psalm 18

129

What more do I need

My Lord, my shepherd
What more do I need?
You give me rest
You give me peace
You give me strength

ROBERT HICKS

You guide me every day
Even in the darkest time
With you near
I will not be afraid
My critics will be confused
When they see your miracles
I feel like an honoured guest
With my cup being continually filled
What goodness, what love
I have for all my life
Your house is my home
For ever and ever
From Psalm 23

How long will I live?

My mind is restless
But the more I think
The more troubled I become
I cannot keep asking myself
How long will I live?
Lord when will I die?
Tell me how soon will death come
How short you have made my life
To me, my lifetime seems nothing
What then can I hope for?
I must put my hope in you Lord
Hear my prayers

JOYCE

Listen to me cry
Come to my aid even when I weep
From Psalm 39

Strength in weakness

Who is there to help
In times of trouble?
God is
He is both a shelter from the storm
And strength when weakness takes over.
From Psalm 46

Praise and Praise again

Praise God for who He is
Praise God for what He has done
Praise God with all your strength
Praise God with the music of your heart
Praise God with the harmony of your life
From Psalm 150

The New Life-Body

Good News

This is Good News
That's why it's worth repeating
That's why faith keeps you strong
Christ did die for our sins.

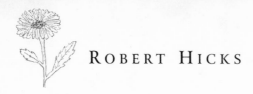

Christ was buried
Christ was raised
Christ did appear alive

No message, No hope

It is the truth
It is the Good News
For if Christ did not rise
How can His followers rise
If there is no resurrection
We have no message to offer
No message of Good News
Our faith is a delusion
We still have our sin!

The New Way

What a truth this is
Christ has been raised, the ultimate guarantee,
That sleep in death gives way on the ressurection day
Adam was one way, the way of death for all
Christ is the new way, the way of life, a life for heaven
This is your guarantee
For death no longer wins. For death itself will die.

JOYCE

Our new body

> *Think now of your hope – A new life – A new body,*
> *Like a seed sown into the ground, it dies*
> *But only too soon to burst into life*
> *A new life with a New Body*
> *When you sow a seed, you do not sow the*
>   *New Body*
> *That comes with its New Life,*
> *A new life in its death.*

Created by God

> *The New Body comes from the New Life*
> *A body created and provided by God*
> *All living things need a body*
> *A body to live in their environment*
> *You will have a New Body – a body for your environment,*
> *The environment of heaven.   Your home to live in.*

Powerful - Beautiful - Eternal

> *So now hold onto this.*
> *Yes, your body now is mortal, subject to time*
> *With the New Life Body it is immortal*
> *Yes, your body when buried, is ugly*
> *With the New Life Body it is so beautiful*
> *Yes your body eventually grows weak*
> *With the New Life Body it will always be strong*

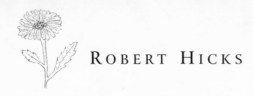

Yes your body is limited by physical desires and needs
With the New Life Body it knows no limitations
It will be spiritual

Heaven Not Earth

This is the resurrection
Adam gave us a body that belongs to the earth
Jesus gives us a body that belongs to heaven
We will definitely be like the one who came from heaven
Just as we wear the likeness of Adam, the man made of
*   earth*
So we will wear the likeness of Jesus, the man from
*   heaven.*

Changed

Listen to this secret truth
We may not all die, but we all will be changed.
It will happen so quick, as quick as the blinking of an eye.
The trumpet will sound, the dead will be raised,
*   to die no more.*
Then we shall be changed, with our New Life Body
*   for heaven*

JOYCE

Victory

Now do you understand?
What is mortal must be changed into what is immortal
What will die must be changed into what can never die
Death then is destroyed, Victory is secured.
Death, what now is your victory?
Death, how now can you hurt?
Death, you have no victory
Death, you have no power.
God has the power,
God has the victory,
Passed on to us in Christ Jesus Our Lord
This should change the way you think
This should change the way you live.
From the first letter to the Corinthians
chapter 15.

135

"A CHILD'S THOUGHTS"

"A CHILD'S THOUGHTS"

When I recollected some of my thinking as a child, which I have scattered throughout my book "A Child Cries", a few kind friends informed me that these "thoughts" had a power of their own, in their raw state and without comment.

THOUGHT PATTERNS WITHOUT WORDS

My only comment therefore, by way of introduction to "A Child's Thoughts" is to say that, because communicating verbally was nearly impossible except for immediate family and a few friends who had learned to understand my peculiar way of speaking, I did spend countless hours every day thinking and reasoning within myself. Indeed, I held conversations with imaginary individuals, or imaginary conversations with real people. This, coupled with the developing powers of observation - that all children are blessed with – is the reason why I have no difficulty in remembering those "Child's Thoughts".

Of course, the adult now in me has occasionally added to the vocabulary, but, looking back, I realise that I did have quite an extensive vocabulary even though I could not read, write or speak, as I should.

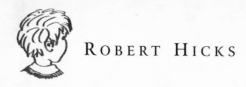

ROBERT HICKS

I do hope this section of the Gift Book will open up your own emotions to the needs of present day children near and far.

1

"No-one can see my tears because they are inside, deep inside, and they hurt."

2

The Slums, the children's homes. Now 'home'. All strange places to live. I wonder what next.

3

"One day, I will be free...! One day, I will be someone...!"

4

"Slumland was a place where a lot of small minded people lived small small lives, but not much smaller than most people outside of slumland. Funny that and a bit sad really."

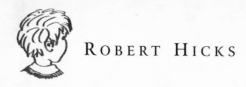
140

5

"All I am to my Mum and Dad is an allowance from the Government and a ration book for food, not their son."

6

"The way for me to overcome not being able to read is page by page and word by word even if it takes years to do it"

7

"I am a stranger at home and an idiot at school, a wild boy outside."

8

"Maybe, one day, I will have someone to help me. Maybe, one day, I will have a friend... but I am not sure. Maybe's are only dreams."

9

"My head is full, my heart is heavy, my speech is wrong, my home is cold, my life is empty. That's me in a nutshell."

10

"What do I want...? ...to be able to talk, to be able to read, to be able to write, to be able to belong, to be able to laugh and to be happy on the inside."

11

"All my life, I have been robbed. But no more."

12

"They do not understand what I am saying. I cannot say what they want me to. I am not the same as other children. If only I could speak the way they want me to!"

13

"I don't like the kitchen at night. It is the worst place in all the world. It is cold and I am all alone with Dad.
I am afraid."

14

"They told me I had a home to go to, but they did not tell me about the kitchen or the bedrooms or my Mom or my Dad."

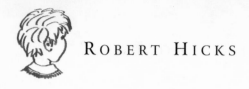

15

"I think I should me happy. Something must be wrong"

16

"I was born in a bombing raid, neglected in the slums,
taken into care with no voice to speak.....
not much to start life with!"

17

"I was her fourth child but she never knew my birthday.
She never knew me - not even for one day in a year."

18

"I don't remember when I was very little but I know I was
never allowed to be 'myself'. I was alone and unloved."

19

"I was told I had a baby sister, but I have never seen her.
I want to see her and in a strange way
I miss her very much."

20

"The men sing loud songs and smell of beer, and then they
are sick and the buckets come out week after week."

21

"Jesus had a manger, I had a cardboard box.
I am glad Jesus wasn't born in a palace."

22

"My first awareness came more in impressions than
thoughts; impressions of an unhappy start in life.
My nostrils rebelled against the vile smells.
My ears closed to the excessively loud noises.
My eyes constantly looked away.
My taste spoiled by grease and lard.
My flesh jerked away from the slightest touch. It was as
though all my senses were at war with their environment,
with no protection from Mother or Father."

23

"I like it here. It's warm and there's hot food and children
to play with and a big woman who smiles.
But I know it won't last."

24

"They offered me a home: they gave me Hell."

25

"Mom has lots of children, but not lots of love.
Maybe no love at all."

26

"Can she be my mother? Is this my real mother who will love
me, talk to me, listen to me and care for me?
No: I don't think she really is my mother!"

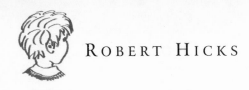

27

"I don't know who I am, why I am here or how long I will
stay here, but I know it's better than where I was before.

That was horrible.

They tell me I can stay for Christmas.

I don't know what Christmas is.

They tell me I will have hot food and lots of presents,
but I don't believe them.

I know somebody will take me away.

I wish I could stop for Christmas and have hot food
and lots of presents."

28

"Today, I walked a long way from the warm Home to a cold
house and it was very, very cold."

29

"I don't like it when it's quiet.
Bad things can happen in the quiet."

30

"I cannot understand why Mom has taken me away from
a warm house and hot food and children to play with and
Christmas. I feel so cold and hungry and I don't think
Christmas is going to come to our house."

31

"What is a friend?

It must be someone who does not expect to gain anything
from you, but wants to be with you whenever he can.

Maybe no-one in the world has a real friend.

I don't think I will ever have a real friend.

I wonder if I could be a real friend to somebody.

One day, I will try."

32

"My sister has a room all to herself. I wish I had a room to
myself, then I could have a bed to myself instead of sharing
it with all my brothers."

33

"They work all the time on their garden. It's as though it is
all they have in the whole world... their garden.

There must be something special about a garden."

34

"I miss my shiny pennies! I miss my bar of chocolate!

I miss my game of hoop-la!

I miss them all.

They were given to me. I had not been given things before."

35

"Other children in the Lane have told me they get cards and
presents for their birthdays.

Only John and Jean have got presents in our house.

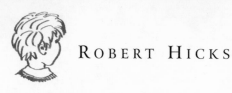

Bernard, Brian and I do not. I wonder why we never get cards or presents. Mom and Dad spend their money when they go out every night. Maybe that's the reason why."

36

"I remember the slums; the smells, the noises and the children. I wish they could all come out into the countryside. Bartley Green is big enough for everyone!"

37

"I went a long walk to where the children play on swings while their mothers talk to each other.
The mothers looked so happy talking and they never seemed to stop. The children looked so happy playing and they never seemed to stop either. I am glad that some families have nice mothers and children.
I wish Dad and Mom would come to the playground and see how happy people can be."

38

"I know how to count the stars in the sky!
I make a circle with my first finger and thumb and stretch it from my eye until I can count a hundred stars. Then I move the circle around the sky and count how many circles it needs to cover the sky.
There are hundreds of hundreds of stars!"

39

"I lived in two places at the same time,
but they were not the same."

40

"I know people think I am crazy because I talk to myself,
but if I don't do it, I will never learn to speak."

41

"I keep humming quietly to myself. I don't know why, but the
vibration from the humming stops the pain from thoughts
I cannot share with anyone. I like thinking, but I wish I could
talk as well."

42

"I can't understand it! I want to be happy in my new home
with all the family, but I don't want to come home until it is
dark, because then I can crawl into bed without Mom or
Dad knowing. I don't think they miss me anyway.
I don't understand it."

43

"The brook is clean, fresh and flowing, and when the sun is
out it is warm. I don't hum when I can hear
the sound of the brook.
Over and over it says, "Tickle, tickle..." I put my feet into
the water and it tickles me.
The birds and I like coming to the brook. It keeps us happy."

44

"The worm doesn't like coming out of the ground because it is dangerous. The birds might eat it. I like getting out of the house because it is safer outside.
The worm stops in the dark, afraid to come into the light.
I stay as long as I can in the light, afraid of going back into the dark house. I am glad I am not a worm, but I wish I was not afraid of the night at home."

45

"The Lane is full of children.
I am so glad this is not the slums."

46

"I like the buttercup and daisy flowers in the fields.
They both have bright yellow eyes looking up, but they close at night time. I feel like the field flowers. When I am out of the house something inside me opens up as I walk the fields talking to myself.
When I get home at night, something inside me closes down and all I can do is hum quietly to myself."

47

"Mom and Dad don't notice me.
Jean never speaks to me; Donald and John do sometimes.
Bernard and Brian talk to each other.
I speak but no-one listens. Most of the time, I talk to myself

in my head. I think I must live inside my head. I wish I could get my thoughts out of my head."

48

"I dreamed again of the red robin
who I trapped in a cage.
I now understand why he kept hurting himself trying to escape from the trap. I now understand why when he escaped, he never came back.
One day, I will escape! One day, I will be free!"

49

"I like it when Dad tells us the stories of the war, but I can't believe that everyone else is bad but us."

50

"The farmer's black and white horses are strong, very strong - much stronger than the farmer. Yet they do everything the farmer tells them to do.
The farmer looks very small by the side of the horses, but they never run away from him, no matter how hard they work or tired they become. I wonder what the secret of the farmer is?"

51

"It's strange to think that in our small village of Bartley Green we had the tallest lady in the world. I wonder where the tallest man is!"

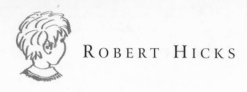

52

"I missed the Sunday hot food today. I must go to school
tomorrow, or I will die without food."

53

"There was a nice song at the Children's Club at the little
'tin hut' church:

"What can I give Him, poor as I am?

If I were a shepherd, I would bring a lamb.

If I were a wise man, I would do my part,

Yet what can I give Him?

Give my heart!"

54

"The stars have been there from the beginning which means
I can see the same stars as anybody else. This makes me the
same as everybody else. I am glad!"

55

"I dreamed today that I was a good boy and that everybody
wanted to talk and to listen to me.

I dreamed I was living in a big house with a big kitchen with
lots of hot food. I know it was only a dream, but I liked it
very much. Maybe, one day, the dream will come true!

But I'm not sure."

56

"What a greater fool I have been, to have spent so long looking in the gutter, when I could have been enjoying God's creation all around me!"

57

"I wish people would smile like Miss Treadwell.

When she smiles at me, I am happy.

When I am happy, I can smile too.

When I smile at Mrs. Taylor next door, she smiles back.

If Mom and Dad could smile, maybe they would be happy.

I smile at them, but most times I don't think they notice me.

One time, Dad said, "What are you grinning at?"

as if I should not be smiling."

58

"I like my teacher, Miss Treadwell. She doesn't talk to me as there are too many of us in the classroom, but she does notice me. When she looks at me, she smiles at me. Mom never looks at me or smiles.

I wish Miss Treadwell was my Mom, but I don't think she would like my Dad."

59

"I don't like taking my 'Free Dinner' tickets to my teacher at school. The tickets tell everyone that my Mom and Dad don't look after me.

I don't like the other children knowing I have free meals.

ROBERT HICKS

They say nasty things and tease me.
But I do like the food. I know I must eat plenty at school as
there is no food at home. I don't want to starve to death!"

60

"The puddings we have at school are tapioca, semolina or
sponge with custard.
I don't like the tapioca - it reminds me of frogs spawn. The
semolina is slimy. I do like the sponge with the hot custard.
I eat all the puddings, even the ones I don't like because
I know there will be nothing to eat at home in the evening."

61

"I like John a lot, but I am also jealous because he can speak
right and play the piano and everybody likes him. I wish
somebody would like me."

62

"We had a big bonfire in front of our house for 'Guy Fawkes
Night'. I was pleased because I collected most of the wood
for burning, walking many miles to find broken branches.
The neighbours like the big fire and cooked their potatoes at
the edge of it. They gave me some potatoes and they tasted
so good! Some children had 'sparklers'.
I wish I had a sparkler."

63

"I don't like the five of us sleeping in the same bed. I wish
I had my own bed, like in the Children's Homes.

152

Donald keeps most of the coat to himself and John keeps
making wheezing noises. I was wet again this morning and
I don't want to keep sleeping in this bed next to my brother
who can't help wetting it. I wish I had my own bed!"

64

"We have everything. We have nothing. It's scary."

65

"The teacher keeps telling me to get my hair cut. I keep
telling my Mom, but she never listens.
When a letter came from the teacher, Mom put a basin
over my head and cut my hair around it using her own
spittle to control the hair.
Now I know why they call it a 'basin cut'.
My hair feels funny so short. It won't be cut again
for a long time."

66

"I went to the 'Saturday Matinee' for the first time today
and was surprised to see how many children were there. The
picture house was full! The children sang lots of songs I had
never heard before. "Hop Along Cassidy" was the hero of
the film and he could always outshoot the bad men, even
when riding fast on his horse. I hope I will become a
cowboy one day."

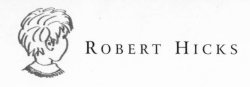
67

"The 'Pictures' fill my mind with so many ideas and help me
forget home. I know it's not real. The films are like my
dreams, but I like them. Maybe, one day, I will have a horse.
Maybe, one day, I will ride away and go anywhere I want to.
Maybe, one day, I will be somebody."

68

"Jean looks funny. Bernard looks funny.
Brian speaks funny. I speak funny.
But it's not funny. It's not fair.
Why can't we just be normal the same as everyone else?"

69

"Tiger, the cat, had kittens in my bed in the night. She came
to me because I am her friend and I hum and she purrs to
me. Dad drowned all the kittens in the morning because we
have no food for them. I keep crying in my heart. Only Tiger
hears me. She looks so sad and has stopped purring and now
cries in 'miaows' for her lost kittens.
Dad has told me I must not let Tiger come in the house
again - but I will."

70

"I wish I could stop dreaming of running around looking for
food and only wearing a short shirt.
I wish Dad and Mom were not always in my dreams eating
my food. I don't like night time."

71

"I am good at Maths in school. I am always at the top of the class. The teacher said I am good enough to be top of the school. I can 'see' the answers without a lot of thinking. Is it because I am thinking all the time? I like Maths, but I wish I could read as well. I can work out numbers easily, but I cannot understand alphabet letters. I do not understand why."

72

"Why can I not speak what is in my mind? When the teacher speaks, I understand. When he gives me books to read and write in, I don't. I wish he would speak more and not give me the books, but I do like looking at the pictures in them."

73

"I am late again for school. Dad made me go up Jiggins Lane to get his newspaper first. The paper is called "The Mirror". The first time I went for it, I thought I was getting a new mirror for the wall to replace the cracked one Dad uses for shaving. The man at the shop insisted that Dad wanted the newspaper. He was right. Dad did not tell me off for bringing a newspaper instead of a mirror, but they caned me at school for being late."

74

"Mr. Woolley wanted to cane me today. He said I had cheated at Maths. I refused to be caned. Mr. Woolley became red in the face. I felt sorry for Mr. Woolley, but it would not be fair for me to be punished for something I did not do. I am always being punished for nothing."

75

"The old oak tree is full of mystery and secrets. It's heart is big enough for three of us and I like to hide inside it or climb up into its branches and see a long way off."

76

"Today, I pulled some of the farmer's carrots out of the ground to eat. I put the green tops back into the soil but I don't think they will grow again. I hope he won't mind me having the carrots, as I am so hungry."

77

"I love the fresh water from the spring that started running when the world began.
I feel so clean inside when I drink it."

78

"I stole a pack of playing cards,
but I don't like playing with them.
It was wrong. I wish I could take them back.
I am sorry for the lonely man who may not have money to buy some more."

79

"New clothes for just one day! I am not surprised to lose them. The big surprise was to have them at all."

80

"I wanted to feel special having time alone with my Mom for a day's outing. But now the day has come, I don't feel special. She doesn't want to talk to me.
She wants to talk to a strange man."

81

"I saw Mom kiss and cuddle a tall black man on the coach coming back from her Works' Outing. I know Mom will leave us one day. She doesn't love Dad or us. She only wanted me with her on the outing so that Dad would not know she was with this man. I saw so many people happy today, including my Mom. I am not happy."

82

"I am ten now but I never get new clothes to keep. One day Mom did get me new clothes that I thought were for me to keep. I wore the suit to go with Mom on her Works' Outing a long way away. I wished the trousers were long instead of short, but it didn't really matter
because I only wore the suit once."

83

"Slowly, I am losing my family. It's like a slow death."

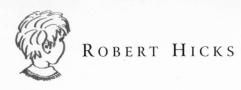

84

"Donald ran away again and now he is in trouble and we
are told we will not see him for a long, long time, if ever.
It's not his fault! It's Mom and Dad's fault!
Why haven't we got a proper Mom and Dad?
It isn't fair that I won't see Donald again."

85

"Mom has stopped cooking a dinner on Sundays and she
spends most of her time back in the city.
I don't know if I really miss her, but I know something
terrible is going to happen."

86

"I cannot hug you, Mom. I cannot! Cannot! Cannot! I don't
want to, because you don't really want to hug me or be near
me or understand me. You're always saying you'll leave us
and I know you will one day. But it's cold at night and we
need your coat on our bed."

87

"Why did you say I did not love you, as if it was my fault?
Why did you say you were leaving us all, as if it was our
fault? Why did you want to say, 'Goodbye'?"

88

"Mom... I don't understand why you have run away and not
taken Jean with you!
Jean is now the only girl, all alone and afraid."

89

"John... I am so pleased you are my big brother.
I need you. Please don't go away as well."

90

"Today I only got dry sandwiches. I was expecting hot food
like I got at the other Children's Home.
I hoped that nice cuddly lady would be here with her smiling
face but it's a different Home. How I miss her!"

91

"My Mom has gone. My hair has gone.
My clothes have gone. My family has gone.
I am all alone again."

92

"I am still hungry, but now I feel clean inside and out after
the shower and now this bed that smells so nice.
I wonder what will happen next."

93

"I look strange in the grey clothes and they feel so heavy,
but I know they are not really mine.
Children at school also know they don't belong to me and
they make fun of me."

94

"Today, I made friends with the leader of a 'gang'.
He needs a friend. All the boys need a friend.
Inside they are so empty."

ROBERT HICKS

95

"The boys look so sad. They look as if they are always about
to cry. I wish there was someone who could help them."

96

"I played cricket today with John and some other boys.
John was not happy when I 'caught him out'. When it was
my turn to bat, he was not happy because he couldn't get
me 'out' and I wouldn't declare.
The girls who were watching left, so in the end John and the
boys left also.
I was the smallest boy playing and I think I spoiled the game
for them, but I am still pleased with how well I played."

97

"God! God! Why am I imprisoned in this cage so long? The
robin only suffered for a short time and I let him go free as
soon as I saw his distress. Why can I not be free and live a
'normal' life?"

98

"I watched a spider making its web in the bushes. Although
it spends a long time making its web, I know that tomorrow
it will have lots of breaks in it and the spider will start all
over again. The teacher keeps telling me to try and try again
to read. I do keep trying, but I can't see the words on the
page. I really do want to learn to read and, like the spider,
I don't mind trying again... but I just can't see the words on

160

the page. How can other children see the words to read?"
"Mom has gone - but she was never really here.
How I miss her coat!"

99

"I know inside my heart I cry a lot. But no-one can see the
tears. I even cry inside when I am smiling outside.
I don't want them to know I have been crying.
When I grow up, I will never cry again because when I am
an adult no-one will be able to hurt me."

100

"I climbed right high up an electric pylon and heard the
funny whirring sound of the wires. I only did it because the
girls were not talking to me and I wanted them to take
notice. The park keeper saw me and came running and
shouting.
I came down very fast and ran away. Later, he came to our
house and told Dad I could easily have been electrocuted."

101

"The world is spinning round fast
according to the teacher at school.
I have worked out that if I jump high enough, the earth will
spin beneath me and I will land in a place further on.
Maybe I have found a new way of travelling!
The women who live nearby look at me strangely while I test
my new idea."

102

"Today I kept ten shillings that was not mine.
I feel ashamed. Ten shillings is the most money I have ever
had. I spent a few pennies and I really did want to take the
rest back, but I knew I would be in trouble for spending the
pennies. It was not worth having that money that did not
belong to me. It worried me too much. I don't want to get
bad like Dad."

103

"Will I ever have some chocolate again? It is such a long
time since Donald stole my bar of chocolate.
I wonder how much longer I will have to wait."

104

"A lady who lives near school sells toffee apples
at lunch break time.
I sometimes get the 'core' from other children and
sometimes there's a bit of toffee apple left too. I like toffee
apple. I am going to save some pennies
to buy one all to myself.
One day I will have a toffee apple all to myself."

105

"I never know when I come home at night which of my
brothers will be missing or have been sent away again."

106

"I am all alone with Dad and I don't know what I have done
to deserve this."

107

"I had a tomato dip today. It was wonderful!"

108

"I had a cup of coffee today in a china cup
with Mrs. Taylor and a digestive biscuit. I have never tasted
anything so nice before! This is the first time I have ever
had a whole biscuit. I never knew that drinking from a
proper cup and saucer could make a drink taste so nice.
I wish we had cups and saucers and whole biscuits."

109

"Dad wanted my milk-round money that I had saved up.
That's not fair. It's my money.
So I ran away with it to Redditch.
The policeman picked me up the next morning and sent me
back to Selly Oak Police Station. They took me back to Dad.
There is nowhere to go but back to Dad.
I am very sad indeed.
I have no way of getting away."

110

"A boy had a bag of marbles and gave me one to play with
him. In the game, I won all his marbles and his bag, which

163

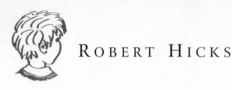

made him cry. I gave him back most of the marbles, including his favourite one and the bag, as I didn't want his mother to come after me. Most of the remaining marbles, I exchanged for comics, leaving me enough to play and win some more to obtain more comics."

111

"I have learned how to write some little words by copying them out of my comics. I have to copy them a lot of times, but I think I can learn words this way. It is hard and it takes a long time. I wish there was an easy way to learn to read and write."

112

"I met a strange man in black today who took my sword of sticks out of my hand and turned it into a cross and then told me I would be a 'soldier of the cross'. He touched my head and blessed me. He had a gentle smile on his face.

After this, he disappeared.

I think he was an angel, but I don't understand why he was in black. I thought angels were always dressed in white."

113

"It was a long walk to the big reservoir and it was getting dark when I got there. I like to look at all the stars reflecting on the water.

By the reservoir, I can talk out loud. No-one is listening or laughing at my strange way of talking.

Here by the reservoir I can think and talk my thoughts out
loud. I also talk to God, but I don't think He listens."

114

"My parents were empty of goodness and love towards their
children, but that emptiness was filled with bad things."

115

"Please, Dad, don't delight in using the belt. Don't get
satisfaction from hurting this child who is of your own seed. "

116

"Night after night, year in year out.
Dad, drunk and cruel... so cruel.
It hurts but no-one knows, nor must they."

117

"Betty has changed. She was kind at first, while Dad was in
prison and I felt noticed. Now she brings different men
home at night with her and I am no longer noticed.
Now I sleep on my own in the cold room again.
I wish Betty had not changed."

118

"I envy Jean coming home because Betty is now giving her
all the attention and is dressing her up to take her to see
the big lights in the City."

119

"Dad came out of prison and hugged me and cried. It was
strange to be hugged by Dad. It has never happened before.

I feel sorry for Dad, but it's his own fault that he went into
prison. I never told anyone that my Dad was in prison."

120

"Jean is never happy and she is always crying and no-one
understands her. She keeps running away, but always comes
back. I feel sorry for her being the only girl at home."

121

"Jean said we should turn the gas on in Dad's bedroom
when he is asleep. I don't know whether she means it.
Things would be happier if Dad was not here and we
belonged to a good family."

122

"I cannot believe what I have seen today.
Brian's leg doesn't look like a boy's leg any more.
I am afraid that someone is going to get killed."

123

"I know what is happening at home is not normal. I know
it is not good. I know it is all wrong.
If only I knew what to do. One day I will."

124

"Ripples from a stone thrown in the reservoir are not
content to stay by the stone, but ripple out until they reach
the edge of their world... I feel the same!

125

"Everything around me is alive, but I don't feel as if I am living. Everything around me is growing. Why am I not growing? It will be a long time before I leave school; maybe then I will start to live and grow. I do very much want to grow as I feel very small."

126

"When I have free school dinner tickets, I feel bad and very poor. But today I have an official 'pass' into the big marquee for a meal that I have earned by working at the fun day and I feel great!

I have never felt like this before
with a meal ticket. It is wonderful!"

127

"Today, the big lady from the N.S.P.C.C. came again with trousers, shirt, coat, mack and shoes for me.
As usual, they are all too big and she tells me that I will grow into them.
I know they will be worn out before I grow into them and I'll probably lose the mack.
I wish I had some proper clothes just for me."

167

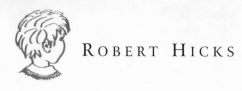
128

"I am on a train for the first time. It's a train with a big powerful engine full of life, pulling lots and lots of carriages carrying so many people - and I am one of them! I can't believe it."

129

"The train is alive and it talks to itself over and over again, as well as making funny noises when it goes through the tunnels. It goes so fast.
I can't believe I am really on this train!"

130

"I am fourteen and grown up, but today I feel like a little child. Here at the seaside I am smelling, feeling and seeing things I have never seen before. I feel fixed to the spot with excitement! I never knew the sea was so big, so powerful! It has touched me... I have felt it and tasted it. It is now inside me and will never leave me."

131

"I am happy in this big house by the sea. The days are going by too fast. I don't want the holiday to end. It is a real Christmas: my first real Christmas ever."

132

"Dad keeps kicking Lassie, and she crawls up to him with her eyes wide open, pleading for him to stop.
Dad's cruel to her. Just because she wet the kitchen floor,

Dad threw her out of the house. I can still hear her whining
outside the door.
I wish Dad would stop kicking Lassie
- it makes me hurt inside."

133

"I have been fighting all my life. This fight is the most
important of all and the most disturbing."

134

"I want to love my Dad and to honour and respect him.
I want to be proud of him. I want other people to know
I have a good father.
I wish... but I know that wishing is no good."

135

"I know so much... but I also know so little.
What I don't know is more important than what I do know.
I am ashamed,
but I must try to learn what I don't yet know."

136

"The water was cool and clean and according to the teacher
it had been running since the moment God made the world.
That is a very very long time. It was here before any trees
or bushes. Yet it is still here now and I can wash my face in
its water and drink it too.
I wish I could drink it every day."

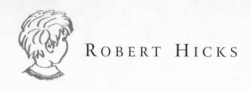

ROBERT HICKS

137

"I am afraid. I am alone. Soon I will have to find a job and look after myself. But first, there is Dad. I have to face my deepest fear... I have to face Dad."

138

"I only have one place at 335 that I can call my own: my corner in the living room. The small cupboard box that covers the gas meter belongs to me."

139

"I know I must fight Dad, but everything inside me is telling me that it's wrong.

But I can't help it, I must fight Dad."

140

"Dad's always saying that Donald and our half-sister Tracey are 'bastards' but he treats us all the same. To him, we are all bastards."

141

"For five years, I never told Dad about Mom and the strange man on the coach. For five years, I kept a dark secret."

142

"I looked through my Dad's eyes into his soul and it was not nice. He was a 'nobody' and he knew it. His life had turned into nothing and I was ashamed and also afraid, not for his life, but for mine."

170

143

"I am no longer a child. I am now a grown up boy, but I hate
the way I became one! I have Dad's blood on my yellow
shirt and I know I will never forget this. I have no love in my
heart for Dad or Mom and I don't really know my brothers
and sister. I am now a grown up boy, but what shall I do
with my life. What I do know is that I must not
become like Dad."

144

"As a child, I cried, but no-one heard me cry.
No-one knew the loneliness, the sense of nothingness that
comes by being betrayed by one's own parents.
The tears are deep, so deep that I sometimes forget until
suddenly they are awakened and I find myself wanting to
cry all over again.
I want the pain to go away.
One day, I will laugh... but first I have to learn to speak.
I must learn to speak.
I must learn to read.
I must learn to live.
I must learn to be me!"

145

"A romantic tale may exaggerate,
but not by diminishing the truth."

As I read my "Child's Thoughts",
I became sad and melancholy
With my head and heart full of sympathy
For the tragic waste
Of so many children throughout the world.

Yet I realise
That if each individual were to help one child,
Directly or indirectly,
The revolution of love that Jesus longed for
Would rescue millions of children.

Nature's beautiful healing properties to body, soul and mind cannot be exaggerated to those whose ears, eyes and heart are open.

- *I was there...* when I watched the farmer's huge horses - one white and one black - straining against the leather thongs that pulled the huge cart balanced on two wheels, with its cargo of hay that seemed to reach right up into the sky.
- *I was there...* inside the old oak tree whose heart in an instant had been ripped out by the force of lightening's power, leaving a gash in its side,

opening a door for me to enter.

- *I was there...* to drink from a crystal pure spring of cold water whose course had never changed and whose journey had commenced at the birth of the earth.

- *I was there...* when a huge neglected damson tree, turned wild, produced an abundance of fruit as large as plums, weighing down the strong branches so that I could hide inside as a secret place.

- *I was there...* when the wild wide stream that separated fields flowed freely on its boundless journey to the ocean, and I would pluck up courage to jump across, knowing that - if I failed - my shoes and feet would be soaked and I would laugh aloud for all nature to hear.

- *I was there...* to feel the wind at play its crazy presence on my face, while my ears tuned in to the melodious sounds of its movements through a myriad leaves on the trees.

- *I was there...* when the bluebells covered the woodland floor so luxuriously and every step I took released a fragrance that filled the air.

- *I was there...* walking along hedgerows older than nations themselves, observing the birds in their nests, touching but never stealing their precious eggs.

- *I was there...* lying on my back, chewing on the stringy lengths of green grass as my imagination made caricatures of the fluffy white clouds moving to and fro.

- *I was there...* climbing proud trees and from a height gazing all around like a young prince surveying his future kingdom.

- *I was there...* when what seemed like ten thousand times ten thousand assembled birds swooped around, filling the skies, preparing for their long journey away from our winter and into warmer climates.

- *I was there...* when cows chewed the green grass and little lambs skipped in the spring and rabbits peered out of their burrows, challenging me to run after them, which I did!

- *I was there...* when the farmer hand-baled his hay in traditional stacks with a 'dolly head' to crown each one, before the machines undertook the task but could only produce a standard cuboid brick of hay.

- *I was there...* when there was no artificial light to dim the clear skies at night and the heavens were filled with billions of sparkling eyes, each one winking like a diamond - just for me.

- *I was there...* when the strong horse chestnut tree dropped its seeds, huge shiny conkers encased in spiky protecting balls; conkers through which we could bore holes to thread string for boyish games.

- *I was there...* a child from the slums and there was nothing among the slums and squalor that had prepared me for such a glorious sight and experience.

- *I was there...* aware of the miracle in nature to calm and to heal. It can enrich the soul of anyone who has eyes to see and ears to hear and a heart to respond. I know!... for I was there!

- *I was there...* a child who possessed nothing; a 'nobody' with no adult taking an interest in me. Yet nothing can take away the riches that I enjoyed in the wide expanse of the countryside. Every sense and sensation that had been violated in the slums was revived. Every nerve of the human body regained its sensitivity and eagerly nourished itself in the successive galleries of splendour and glory displayed by the seasons of nature.

- *I was there...* at one with nature, like a baby clinging to his mother's breast.

- *I was there...* like an innocent child learning to crawl, to walk, to run, to dance, to whisper, to

175

speak, to shout!

- *I was there...* in a kingdom fit for any king, the birthright of every child who enters our world.

- *I was there!*

I wonder, "Would you like to go down into the fields and woods today?" Because if so, you will be in for 'a big surprise'! If you visit the Midlands, which is at the heart of England, why not include Woodgate Valley Park? It is still there, exhaling fresh air from its huge lungs to the residents of 'two villages' which are now part of one city: Birmingham.

MIRACLE WORDS

MIRACLE WORDS

In this final section, I have included 365 amazing verses from the Holy Bible. Most of these verses are taken from the 400-year-old translation that I copied in my youth, in order to overcome my inability to read, write and speak, following my operation of being tongue-tied. Little did I realise I would also overcome a major part of being dyslexic at the time.

If you have time, you may find it useful to read in your own Bible the entire Chapter that is indicated. For most people, that will be a modern translation.

Many times, individuals come to me requesting help in reading this book, as it looks at first such a huge book of around 1,300 pages.

I tell them that it is not one book, but in actual fact a library of books in two parts: the Old Testament and the New Testament. There are 66 books in all, and they have been divided into Chapters and, in most modern translations, also put into sections with Headings and sub-Headings.

My advice is therefore to read the Bible, "a bit, and often." If you have never read the Holy Bible, may that is a good way for you to start.

If you find a regular time to read, why not select one Chapter and look for one verse there which you can copy out by hand into your Diary or Notebook. Undoubtedly, copying out the Bible by hand helped me to appreciate this "Miracle Book".

I have met a few people who have been inspired by worthy individuals or courageous events. In contrast, the number of individuals who have been inspired by reading God's Word on a regular basis runs into millions and millions, all around the globe, and you might find this to be true also for you.

Happy reading!

JANUARY 1st

Be strong and of good courage; be not afraid, neither
be thou dismayed: for the Lord thy God is with thee
whithersoever thou goest.

Joshua 1:9

JANUARY 2nd

O Lord our Lord, how excellent is thy name
in all the earth!

Psalm 8:1

JANUARY 3rd

Let your light so shine before men, that they may see
your good works, and glorify your Father which
is in heaven.

Matthew 5:16

JANUARY 4th

Thou art worthy, O Lord, to receive glory and honour
and power: for thou hast created all things.

Revelation 4:11

JANUARY 5th

To all who received him, to those who believed in his
name, he gave the right to become children of God.

John 1:12 (NIV)

JANUARY 6th

In (Christ) and through him, we may approach
God with confidence.

Ephesians 3:12 (NIV)

JANUARY 7th

God be merciful unto us, and bless us; and cause his
face to shine upon us.

Psalm 67:1

JANUARY 8th

In all things God works for the good of those who
love him.

Romans 8:28 (NIV)

JANUARY 9th

He that converteth the sinner from the error of his
way shall save a soul from death, and shall hide a
multitude of sins.

James 5:20

JANUARY 10th

He has rescued us from the dominion of darkness
and brought us into the kingdom of the Son he loves.

Colossians 1:13 (NIV)

JANUARY 11th

For whom the Lord loveth he correcteth;
even as a father the son in whom he delighteth.

Proverbs 3:12

JANUARY 12th

Jesus findeth Philip and saith unto him, Follow me.

John 1:43

JANUARY 13th

O worship the Lord in the beauty of holiness:
fear before him, all the earth.

Psalm 96:9

JANUARY 14th

183

Go ye therefore and teach all nations, baptizing them
in the name of the Father, and of the Son, and of the
Holy Ghost.

Matthew 28:19

JANUARY 15th

I can do all things through Christ which
strengtheneth me.

Philippians 4:13

JANUARY 16th

Now faith is the substance of things hoped for,
the evidence of things not seen.

Hebrews 11:1

JANUARY 17th

Come now, and let us reason together, saith the Lord:
though your sins be as scarlet, they shall be white as
snow.

Isaiah 1:18

JANUARY 18th

Holy Father, protect them by the power of your name
– the name you gave me – so that they may be one,
as we are one.

John 17:11 (NIV)

JANUARY 19th

Alleluia: for the Lord God omnipotent reigneth.

Revelation 19:6

JANUARY 20th

By this shall all men know that ye are my disciples,
if ye have love one to another.

John 13:35

JANUARY 21st

There is neither Jew nor Greek, slave nor free, male nor female, for you are all one in Christ Jesus.

Galatians 3:28 (NIV)

JANUARY 22nd

Endeavouring to keep the unity of the Spirit in the bond of peace.

Ephesians 4:3

JANUARY 23rd

Ye were as sheep going astray; but are now returned unto the Shepherd and Bishop of your souls.

1 Peter 2:25

JANUARY 24th

Trust in the Lord with all thy heart; and lean not unto thine own understanding.

Proverbs 3:5

JANUARY 25th

Christ Jesus came into the world to save sinners, of whom I am the chief.

1 Timothy 1:15

JANUARY 26th

Be strong in the grace that is in Christ Jesus.

2 Timothy 2:1

JANUARY 27th

Answer me because of your great love,
because you keep your promise to save.

Psalm 69:13 (GNB)

JANUARY 28th

The same Lord is Lord of all and richly blesses all
who call on him.

Romans 10:12 (NIV)

JANUARY 29th

If we believe that Jesus died and rose again, even so
them also that sleep in Jesus will God bring with him.

1 Thessalonians 4:14

JANUARY 30th

Thanks be to God, which giveth us the victory
through our Lord Jesus Christ.

1 Corinthians 15:57

JANUARY 31st

To whom then will ye liken me, or shall I be equal?
saith the Holy One.

Isaiah 40:25

FEBRUARY 1st

Blessing, and honour, and glory, and power, be unto
him that sitteth upon the throne, and to the Lamb
for ever and ever.

Revelation 5:13

FEBRUARY 2nd

Because he himself suffered when he was tempted,
he is able to help those who are being tempted.

Hebrews 2:18

187

FEBRUARY 3rd

As a father pitieth his children, so the Lord pitieth
them that fear him. For he knoweth our frame;
he remembereth that we are dust.

Psalm 103:13-14

FEBRUARY 4th

For God sent not his Son into the world to condemn the world; but that the world through him might be saved.

John 3:17

FEBRUARY 5th

We do not know what we ought to pray for, but the Spirit himself intercedes for us with groans that words cannot express.

Romans 8:26 (NIV)

FEBRUARY 6th

Be patient, then, brothers, until the Lord's coming.

James 5:8 (NIV)

188

FEBRUARY 7th

Be ye kind one to another, tender-hearted, forgiving one another, even as God for Christ's sake hath forgiven you.

Ephesians 4:32

FEBRUARY 8th

A gossip betrays a confidence, but a trustworthy man keeps a secret.

Proverbs 11:13 (NIV)

FEBRUARY 9th

Woe is unto me, if I preach not the gospel!

1 Corinthians 9:16

FEBRUARY 10th

Delight thyself also in the Lord; and he shall give thee the desires of thine heart.

Psalm 37:4

FEBRUARY 11th

Inasmuch as ye have done it unto one of the least of these my brethren, ye have done it unto me.

Matthew 25:40

FEBRUARY 12th

Behold the Lord's hand is not shortened, that it cannot save; neither his ear heavy, that it cannot hear.

Isaiah 59:1

189

FEBRUARY 13th

Humble yourselves therefore under the mighty hand of God, that he may exalt you in due time.

1 Peter 5:6

FEBRUARY 14th

Love is patient, love is kind. It does not envy,
it does not boast, it is not proud.

1 Corinthians 13:4 (NIV)

FEBRUARY 15th

He that trusteth in his riches shall fall: but the
righteous shall flourish as a branch.

Proverbs 11:28

FEBRUARY 16th

Do you not know that in a race all the runners run,
but only one gets the prize? Run in such a way as to
get the prize.

1 Corinthians 9:24 (NIV)

FEBRUARY 17th

The fear of the Lord is the beginning of wisdom:
a good understanding have they that do his
commandments.

Psalm 111:10

FEBRUARY 18th

Whosoever shall smite thee on the right cheek,
turn to him the other also.

Matthew 5:39

FEBRUARY 19th

Abhor that which is evil; cling to that which is good.

Romans 12:9

FEBRUARY 20th

He that hath the Son hath life; and he that hath not
the Son of God hath not life.

1 John 5:12

FEBRUARY 21st

I have been crucified with Christ and... the life I live
in the body I live by faith in the Son of God who
loved me and gave himself for me.

Galatians 2:20 (NIV)

FEBRUARY 22nd

Whosoever loveth instruction loveth knowledge:
but he that hateth reproof is brutish.

Proverbs 12:1

FEBRUARY 23rd

(Christ) is before all things, and in him all things
hold together.

Colossians 1:17 (NIV)

FEBRUARY 24th

O taste and see that the Lord is good:
blessed is the man that trusteth in him.

Psalm 34:8

FEBRUARY 25th

In the world ye shall have tribulation:
but be of good cheer; I have overcome the world.

John 16:33

FEBRUARY 26th

We brought nothing into the world, and we can take
nothing out of it. But if we have food and clothing,
we will be content with that.

1 Timothy 6:7-8 (NIV)

192

FEBRUARY 27th

Endure hardship as discipline;
God is treating you as sons.

Hebrews 12:7

FEBRUARY 28th

Hast thou not heard, that the everlasting God, the
Lord, the creator of the ends of the earth, fainteth
not, neither is weary?

Isaiah 40:28

MARCH 1st

The Lamb...shall lead them unto living fountains of waters: And God shall wipe away all tears from their eyes.

Revelation 7:17

MARCH 2nd

For we preach not ourselves by Christ Jesus the Lord; and ourselves your servants for Jesus' sake.

2 Corinthians 4:5

MARCH 3rd

Ye were sometimes darkness, but now ye are light in the Lord: walk as children of light.

Ephesians 5:8

MARCH 4th

Shall we go on sinning, that grace may increase? By no means! We died to sin; how can we live in it any longer?

Romans 6:2-3 (NIV)

MARCH 5th

Purge me with hyssop, and I shall be clean: wash me, and I shall be whiter than snow.

Psalm 51:7

193

MARCH 6th

As ye have so received Christ Jesus the Lord,
so walk ye in him.

Colossians 2:6

MARCH 7th

Be completely humble and gentle; be patient,
bearing with one another in love.

Ephesians 4:2 (NIV)

MARCH 8th

I have learned the secret of being content in any and
every situation, whether well-fed or hungry, whether
living in plenty or in want.

Philippians 4:12 (NIV)

194

MARCH 9th

The time is fulfilled, and the kingdom of God is at
hand: repent ye, and believe the gospel.

Mark 1:15

MARCH 10th

Christ also hath suffered for sins, the just for the
unjust, that he might bring us to God.

1 Peter 3:18

MARCH 11th

Let us lay aside every weight, and the sin which doth so easily beset us, and let us run with patience the race that is set before us.

Hebrews 12:1

MARCH 12th

Give to him that asketh thee, and from him that would borrow of thee, turn not thou away.

Matthew 5:42

MARCH 13th

If any of you lack wisdom, let him ask of God ...and it shall be given him.

James 1:5

MARCH 14th

My word...will not return to me empty, but will accomplish what I desire.

Isaiah 55:11 (NIV)

MARCH 15th

Create in me a clean heart, O God;
and renew a right spirit within me.

Psalm 51:10

MARCH 16th

Whosoever will come after me, let him deny himself,
and take up his cross, and follow me.

Mark 8:34

MARCH 17th

There is a way that seemeth right unto a man,
but the end thereof are the ways of death.

MARCH 18th

Proverbs 14:12

The world passeth away, and the lust thereof;
but he that doeth the will of God abideth for ever.

1 John 2:17

MARCH 19th

I will maintain my love to him for ever,
and my covenant with him will never fail.

Psalm 89:28 (NIV)

MARCH 20th

As we have opportunity, let us do good unto all men,
especially unto them who are of the household
of faith.

Galatians 6:10

MARCH 2ist

Remember now thy creator in the days of thy youth,
while the evil years come not,
nor the years draw nigh.

Ecclesiastes 12:1

MARCH 22nd

Faithful is he that calleth you, who also will do it.

1 Thessalonians 5:24

197

MARCH 23rd

The preaching of the cross is to them that perish
foolishness; but unto us which are saved
it is the power of God.

1 Corinthians 1:18

MARCH 24th

The Lord shall preserve thy going out and thy coming in from this time forth, and even for evermore.

Psalm 121:8

MARCH 25th

Behold the handmaid of the Lord;
be it unto me according to thy word.

Luke 1:38

MARCH 26th

Share with God's people who are in need.
Practise hospitality.

Romans 12:13 (NIV)

MARCH 27th

Now unto the King eternal, immortal, invisible, the only wise God, be honour and glory for ever and ever.

1 Timothy 1:17

MARCH 28th

One day is with the Lord as a thousand years, and a thousand years as one day.

2 Peter 3:8

MARCH 29th

A fool will believe anything;
sensible people watch their step.

Proverbs 14:15 (GNB)

MARCH 30th

God so loved the world, that he gave his only
begotten Son, that whosoever believeth in him
should not perish, but have everlasting life.

John 3:16

MARCH 31st

Though I walk through the valley of the shadow
of death, I will fear no evil: for thou art with me;
thy rod and thy staff they comfort me.

Psalm 23:4

APRIL 1st

For ye shall hear of wars and rumours of wars:
see that ye be not troubled: for all these things must
come to pass, but the end is not yet.

Matthew 24:6

APRIL 2nd

Praise our God, all ye his servants,
and ye that fear him, both small and great.

Revelation 19:5

APRIL 3rd

Unto every one of us is given grace according
to the measure of the gift of Christ.

Ephesians 4:7

APRIL 4th

You need to persevere, so that when you have done
the will of God, you will receive what he has
promised.

Hebrews 10:36 (NIV)

APRIL 5th

All a man's motives seem innocent to him,
but motives are weighed by the Lord.

Proverbs 16:2 (NIV)

APRIL 6th

If any man serve me, let him follow me...
if any man serve me, him will my Father honour.

John 12:26

APRIL 7th

Except the Lord build the house, they labour in vain
that build it: except the Lord keep the city, the
watchman waketh but in vain.

Psalm 127:1

APRIL 8th

Be ye all of one mind, having compassion one
of another, love as brethren...be courteous.

1 Peter 3:8

APRIL 9th

If we confess our sins, he is faithful and just
to forgive us our sins, and to cleanse us from
all unrighteousness.

1 John 1:9

APRIL 10th

The wolf also shall dwell with the lamb, and the
leopard shall lie down with the kid...
and a little child shall lead them.

Isaiah 11:6

APRIL 11th

Blessed is the man that endureth temptation: for
when he is tried, he shall receive the crown of life,
which the Lord hath promised to them that love him.

James 1:12

APRIL 12th

Commit to the Lord whatever you do,
and your plans will succeed.

Proverbs 16:3 (NIV)

APRIL 13th

Hosanna! Blessed is he who comes in the name
of the Lord!

John 12:13 (NIV)

202

APRIL 14th

Christ is the mediator of a new covenant,
that those who are called may receive the promised
eternal inheritance.

Hebrews 9:15 (NIV)

APRIL 15th

He that glorieth, let him glory in the Lord.

1 Corinthians 1:31

APRIL 16th

Consider him that endured such contradiction of sinners against himself, lest ye be wearied and faint in your minds.

Hebrews 12:3

APRIL 17th

If I then, your Lord and Master, have washed your feet; ye also ought to wash one another's feet.

John 13:14

APRIL 18th

All we like sheep have gone astray; we have turned every one to his own way; and the Lord hath laid on him the iniquity of us all.

Isaiah 53:6

203

APRIL 19th

The end of all things is near. Therefore be clear minded and self-controlled so that you can pray.

1 Peter 4:7 (NIV)

APRIL 20th

Ye seek Jesus of Nazareth, which was crucified: he is risen.

Mark 16:6

APRIL 21st

If ye then be risen with Christ, seek those things
which are above, where Christ sitteth on the right
hand of God.

Colossians 3:1

APRIL 22nd

Love your enemies, bless them that curse you,
do good to them that hate you.

Matthew 5:44

APRIL 23rd

If the world hate you, ye know that it hated me
before it hated you.

John 15:18

APRIL 24th

Be not deceived; God is not mocked: for whatsoever
a man soweth, that shall he also reap.

Galatians 6:7

APRIL 25th

He that shall endure unto the end,
the same shall be saved.

Mark 13:13

APRIL 26th

Better is a little with righteousness than great revenues without right.

Proverbs 16:8

APRIL 27th

Jesus stood in the midst, and saith unto them, Peace be unto you.

John 20:19

APRIL 28th

The Lord is my shepherd; I shall not want.
He maketh me to lie down in green pastures:
he leadeth me beside still waters.

Psalm 23:1-2

205

APRIL 29th

And so shall we ever be with the Lord.

1 Thessalonians 4:17

APRIL 30th

I exhort therefore, that, first of all, supplications, prayers, intercessions, and giving of thanks, be made for all men.

1 Timothy 2:1

MAY 1st

He that believeth on me, the works that I do shall he
do also; and greater works than these shall he do;
because I go to the Father.

John 14:12

MAY 2nd

God shall wipe away all tears from their eyes;
and there shall be no more death, neither sorrow nor
crying... for the former things are passed away.

Revelation 21:4

MAY 3rd

There is a friend that sticketh closer than a brother.

Proverbs 18:24

MAY 4th

Behold, what manner of love the Father hath
bestowed upon us, that we should be called
the sons of God.

1 John 3:1

MAY 5th

You discern my going out and my lying down:
you are familiar with all my ways.

Psalm 139:3 (NIV)

MAY 6th

Be ye therefore perfect, even as your Father
which is in heaven is perfect.

Matthew 5:48

MAY 7th

We also rejoice in our sufferings, because we know
that suffering produces perseverance.

Romans 5:3 (NIV)

MAY 8th

Serve wholeheartedly, as if you were serving the Lord,
not men, because you know that the Lord will reward
everyone for what good he does.

Ephesians 6:7 (NIV)

207

MAY 9th

Lie not one to another, seeing that ye have put off
the old man with his deeds; and have put on the new
man which is renewed.

Colossians 3:9-10

MAY 10th

He that hath pity on the poor lendeth to the Lord.

Proverbs 19:17

MAY 11th

I am the good shepherd: the good shepherd giveth
his life for the sheep.

John 10:11

MAY 12th

Whatsoever things are true, whatsoever things are
honest, whatsoever things are pure, whatsoever things
are lovely...think on these things.

Philippians 4:8

MAY 13th

Submit yourselves to God. Resist the devil,
and he will flee from you.

James 4:7

MAY 14th

As the Father hath loved me, so have I loved you:
continue ye in my love.

John 15:9

MAY 15th

Greater love hath no man than this, that a man lay
down his life for his friends. Ye are my friends, if ye
do whatsoever I command you.

John 15:13

MAY 16th

The people that walked in darkness have seen a great light: they that dwell in the land of the shadow of death, upon them hath the light shined.

Isaiah 9:2

MAY 17th

A gossip betrays a confidence; so avoid a man who talks too much.

Proverbs 20:19 (NIV)

MAY 18th

Abide in me, and I in you. As the branch cannot bear fruit of itself, except it abide in the vine; no more can ye, except ye abide in me.

John 15:4

209

MAY 19th

The Lord also will be a refuge for the oppressed, a refuge in times of trouble.

Psalm 9:9

MAY 20th

Whoever humbles himself like this child is the greatest in the kingdom of heaven.

Matthew 18:5 (NIV)

MAY 21st

Do not take revenge, my friends,
but leave room for God's wrath.

Romans 12:19 (NIV)

MAY 22nd

Those who suffer according to God's will should
commit themselves to their faithful Creator and
continue to do good.

1 Peter 4:19 (NIV)

MAY 23rd

If we live in the Spirit, let us also walk in the Spirit.

Galatians 5:25

MAY 24th

To do justice...is more acceptable to the Lord than
sacrifice.

Proverbs 21:3

MAY 25th

For this is the love of God, that we keep
his commandments: and his commandments
are not grievous.

1 John 5:3

MAY 26th

The Lord is gracious, and full of compassion;
slow to anger, and of great mercy.

Psalm 145:8

MAY 27th

You know very well that the day of the Lord will
come like a thief in the night.

MAY 28th

1 Thessalonians 5:2 (NIV)

For as the heavens are higher than the earth, so are
my ways higher than your ways, and my thoughts
than your thoughts.

Isaiah 55:9

211

MAY 29th

(God) raised him from the dead and seated him at
his right hand in the heavenly realms, far above all
rule and authority, power and dominion.

Ephesians 1:20-21 (NIV)

MAY 30th

Seeing then that we have a great high priest,
that is passed into the heavens, Jesus the Son of God,
let us hold fast our profession.

Hebrews 4:14

MAY 31st

He that is mighty hath done to me great things;
and holy is his name.

Luke 1:49

JUNE 1st

And this is eternal life, that they might
know thee the only true God,
and Jesus Christ whom thou hast sent.

John 17:3

JUNE 2nd

FBlessed is the man that walketh not in the counsel
of the ungodly...his delight is in the law of the Lord.

Psalm 1:1-2

JUNE 3rd

I am the Alpha and Omega, the Beginning and the End. To him who is thirsty I will give to drink without cost from the spring of the water of life.

Revelation 21:6 (NIV)

JUNE 4th

Now unto him that is able to do exceedingly abundantly above all that we ask or think...be glory in the church by Christ Jesus throughout all ages.

Ephesians 3:20

JUNE 5th

Put on therefore... kindness, humbleness of mind, meekness, longsuffering; forbearing one another and forgiving one another.

Colossians 3:12-13

JUNE 6th

If ye have faith as a grain of mustard seed... nothing shall be impossible unto you.

Matthew 17:20

JUNE 7th

Neither give place to the devil... And grieve not the holy Spirit of God, whereby ye are sealed unto the day of redemption.

Ephesians 4:27,30

JUNE 8th

When he, the Spirit of truth, is come, he will guide you into all truth.

John 16:13

JUNE 9th

Having believed in him, you were marked in him with a seal, the promised Holy Spirit, who is a deposit guaranteeing our inheritance.

Ephesians 1:13-14 (NIV)

JUNE 10th

A little sleep, a little slumber, a little folding of the hands to sleep: so shall thy poverty come.

Proverbs 6:10-11

JUNE 11th

(Barnabas) was a good man, and full of the Holy Ghost and of faith.

Acts 11:24

JUNE 12th

Jesus Christ, the same yesterday, today and for ever.

Hebrews 13:8

JUNE 13th

Seek ye the Lord while he may be found,
call ye upon him while he is near.

Isaiah 55:6

JUNE 14th

The fear of the Lord is the beginning of wisdom:
and the knowledge of the holy is understanding.

Proverbs 9:10

JUNE 15th

One cried unto another, and said, Holy, holy, holy is
the Lord of hosts: the whole earth is full of his glory.

Isaiah 6:3

JUNE 16th

I laid me down and slept; I awaked;
for the Lord sustained me.

Psalm 3:5

JUNE 17th

Each one should use whatever gift he has received to serve others, faithfully administering God's grace in its various forms.

1 Peter 4:10 (NIV)

JUNE 18th

Wherefore, my beloved brethren, let every man be swift to hear, slow to speak, slow to wrath.

James 1:19

JUNE 19th

(Jesus said) I am the living bread that came down from heaven: if any man eat of this bread, he shall live for ever.

John 6:51

JUNE 20th

There is no fear in love; but perfect love casteth out fear.

1 John 4:18

JUNE 21st

The more you talk, the more likely you are to sin. If you are wise, you will keep quiet.

Proverbs 10:19 (GNB)

JUNE 22nd

And (Jesus) arose, and rebuked the wind, and said
unto the sea, Peace, be still. And the wind ceased,
and there was a great calm.

Mark 4:39

JUNE 23rd

I tell you, now is the time of God's favour,
now is the day of salvation.

2 Corinthians 6:2 (NIV)

JUNE 24th

Prepare ye the way of the Lord, make straight in the
desert a highway for our God.

Isaiah 40:3

JUNE 25th

If ye forgive men their trespasses, your heavenly
father will also forgive you.

Matthew 6:14

JUNE 26th

He shall feed his flock like a shepherd: he shall gather
the lambs with his arm...and shall gently lead those
that are with young.

Isaiah 40:11

JUNE 27th

Everything God created is good, and nothing is to be
rejected if it is received with thanksgiving.

1 Timothy 4:4 (NIV)

JUNE 28th

When pride comes, then comes disgrace,
but with humility comes wisdom.

Proverbs 11:2 (NIV)

JUNE 29th

Simon Peter answered and said, Thou art the Christ,
the Son of the living God.

Matthew 16:16

JUNE 30th

Search me, O God, and know my heart:
try me, and know my thoughts.

Psalm 139:23

JULY 1st

Let him that is athirst come. And whosoever will,
let him take the water of life freely.

Revelation 22:17

218

JULY 2nd

I am not ashamed of the gospel of Christ:
for it is the power of God unto salvation to every one
that believeth.

Romans 1:16

JULY 3rd

Be not faithless, but believing.

John 20:27

JULY 4th

Let the peace of Christ rule in your hearts,
since as members of one body you were called
to peace. And be thankful.

Colossians 3:15 (NIV)

219

JULY 5th

A righteous man cares for the needs of his animal,
but the kindest acts of the wicked are cruel.

Proverbs 12:10 (NIV)

JULY 6th

(Jesus) instructed them that they should take nothing
for their journey except a staff – no bread,
no haversack, no coppers for their purses.

Mark 6:8 (JB)

JULY 7th

The Lord is my rock, and my fortress, and my deliverer; my God, my strength, in whom I trust.

Psalm 18:2

JULY 8th

At the name of Jesus every knee should bow...
and that every tongue should confess that
Jesus Christ is Lord.

Philippians 2:10-11

JULY 9th

We have not an high priest which cannot be touched with the feeling of our infirmities; but was in all points tempted like as we are, yet without sin.

Hebrews 4:15

JULY 10th

Whether you turn to the right or to the left your ears will hear a voice behind you, saying,
"This is the way, walk in it."

Isaiah 30:21 (NIV)

JULY 11th

Lay up for yourselves treasures in heaven, where neither moth nor rust doth corrupt, and where thieves do not break through nor steal.

Matthew 6:19

JULY 12th

A generous man will prosper; he who refreshes others will himself be refreshed.

Proverbs 11:25 (NIV)

JULY 13th

He hath chosen us in him before the foundation of the world, that we should be holy and without blame before him in love.

Ephesians 1:4

221

JULY 14th

O give thanks unto the Lord; for he is good: his mercy endureth for ever.

Psalm 136:1

JULY 15th

Whosoever drinketh of the water that I shall give him shall never thirst.

John 4:14

JULY 16th

(In) his own self bare our sins in his own body on
the tree, that we, being dead to sins,
should live unto righteousness.

1 Peter 2:24

JULY 17th

God, the blessed and only Ruler, the King of kings
and Lord of lords, who alone is immortal and lives
in unapproachable light.

1 Timothy 6:15-16 (NIV)

JULY 18th

If anyone gives even a cup of cold water to one of
these little ones because he is my disciple...
he will certainly not lose his reward.

Matthew 10:42 (NIV)

JULY 19th

Guard your steps when you go to the house of God.
Go near to listen rather than to offer the sacrifice
of fools.

Ecclesiastes 5:1

222

JULY 20th

Come ye yourselves apart into a desert place,
and rest a while.

Mark 6:31

JULY 21st

Let us therefore follow after the things which make
for peace, and things wherewith one may edify
another.

Romans 14:19

JULY 22nd

If any man be in Christ, he is a new creature:
old things are passed away; behold,
all things have become new.

2 Corinthians 5:17

223

JULY 23rd

He that spareth the rod hateth his son:
but he that loveth him chastises him betimes.

Proverbs 13:24

JULY 24th

For this purpose the Son of God was manifested,
that he might destroy the works of the devil.

1 John 3:8

JULY 25th

Whoever wants to become great among you
must be your servant.

Matthew 20:26 (NIV)

JULY 26th

I pray God your whole spirit and soul and body
be preserved blameless unto the coming of our
Lord Jesus Christ.

1 Thessalonians 5:23

JULY 27th

I pray that out of his glorious riches he may
strengthen you with power through his Spirit
in your inner being.

Ephesians 3:16 (NIV)

JULY 28th

The law of the Lord is perfect, converting the soul:
the testimony of the Lord is sure,
making wise the simple.

Psalm 19:7

JULY 29th

Martha, thou art careful and troubled about many things: But one thing is needful: and Mary hath chosen that good part, which shall not be taken away from her.

Luke 10:41-42

JULY 30th

Ye have not chosen me, but I have chosen you, and ordained you, that ye should go and bring forth fruit, and that your fruit should remain.

John 15:16

JULY 31st

He hath borne our griefs, and carried our sorrows: yet we did esteem him stricken, smitten of God, and afflicted.

Isaiah 53:4

AUGUST 1st

(God) will dwell with them, and they shall be his people, and God himself shall be with them, and be their God.

Revelation 21:3

AUGUST 2nd

He that despiseth his neighbour sinneth: but he that hath mercy on the poor, happy is he.

Proverbs 14:21

AUGUST 3rd

This is the work of God, that ye believe on him whom he hath sent.

John 6:29

AUGUST 4th

The earth is the Lord's, and the fullness thereof; the world, and they that dwell therein.

Psalm 24:1

AUGUST 5th

For all have sinned, and come short of the glory of God; being justified freely by his grace through the redemption that is in Christ Jesus.

Romans 3:23-24

AUGUST 6th

There came a voice out of the cloud, saying, This is my beloved Son: hear him.

Luke 9:35

AUGUST 7th

When Christ, who is your life, shall appear,
then shall ye also appear with him in glory.

Colossians 3:4

AUGUST 8th

Now the God of peace, that brought again from the
dead our Lord Jesus...make you perfect in every good
work to do his will.

Hebrews 13:20-21

AUGUST 9th

A heart at peace gives life to the body,
but envy rots the bones.

Proverbs 14:30 (NIV)

227

AUGUST 10th

Be ye therefore followers of God, as dear children;
and walk in love, as Christ hath also loved us.

Ephesians 5:1-2

AUGUST 11th

Thy word is a lamp unto my feet, and a light unto
my path.

Psalm 119:105

AUGUST 12th

Whosoever shall confess me before men,
him will I confess also before my Father which
is in heaven.

Matthew 10:32

AUGUST 13th

Be strong, fear not: behold, your God will
come...with a recompense; he will come
and save you.

Isaiah 35:4

AUGUST 14th

Honour all men. Love the brotherhood.
Fear God. Honour the king.

1 Peter 2:17

AUGUST 15th

His mercy is on them that fear him from
generation to generation.

Luke 1:50

AUGUST 16th

Better is a little with the fear of the Lord
than great treasure and trouble therewith.

Proverbs 15:16

AUGUST 17th

See then that ye walk circumspectly,
not as fools but as wise, redeeming the time,
because the days are evil.

Ephesians 5:15

AUGUST 18th

He that is without sin among you,
let him cast the first stone at her.

John 8:7

AUGUST 19th

We then that are strong ought to bear the infirmities
of the weak and not to please ourselves.

Romans 15:1

AUGUST 20th

Pray in the Spirit on all occasions with all kinds
of prayers and requests... be alert and always keep
on praying for all the saints.

Ephesians 6:18 (NIV)

AUGUST 21st

God is love; and he that dwelleth in love dwelleth
in God, and God in him.

1 John 4:16

AUGUST 22nd

Walk in the Spirit, and ye shall not fulfil the lust
of the flesh.

Galatians 5:16

AUGUST 23rd

Plans fail for lack of counsel,
but with many advisers they succeed.

Proverbs 15:22 (NIV)

AUGUST 24th

Who is greater? The one who is at the table or the
one who serves? Is it not the one who is at the table?
But I am among you as one who serves.

Luke 22:27 (NIV)

AUGUST 25th

The Lord is my light and my salvation; whom shall
I fear? The Lord is the strength of my life;
of whom shall I be afraid?

Psalm 27:1

AUGUST 26th

No man can serve two masters: for either he will hate
the one, and love the other...
Ye cannot serve God and Mammon.

Matthew 6:24

AUGUST 27th

Know ye not that ye are the temple of God,
and that the Spirit of God dwelleth in you?

1 Corinthians 3:16

AUGUST 28th

By faith Abraham, when he was called to go out
to a place...obeyed; and he went out,
not knowing whither he went.

Hebrews 11:8

AUGUST 29th

The fruit of the Spirit is love, joy, peace,
longsuffering, gentleness, goodness, faith, meekness,
temperance: against such there is no law.

Galatians 5:22-23

AUGUST 30th

He is despised and rejected of men; a man of sorrows and acquainted with grief: and we hid as it were our faces from him.

Isaiah 53:3

AUGUST 31st

Every good gift and every perfect gift is from above, and cometh down from the Father of lights, with whom there is no variableness, neither shadow of turning.

James 1:17

SEPTEMBER 1st

Thy word have I hid in mine heart, that I might not sin against thee.

Psalm 119:11

SEPTEMBER 2nd

Alleluia: for the Lord God omnipotent reigneth. Let us be glad and rejoice, and give honour to him.

Revelation 19:6-7

SEPTEMBER 3rd

Therefore being justified by faith, we have peace
with God through our Lord Jesus Christ.

Romans 5:1

SEPTEMBER 4th

Because of his great love for us, God, who is rich
in mercy, made us alive in Christ even when we were
dead in transgressions.

Ephesians 2:4-5 (NIV)

SEPTEMBER 5th

(Jesus said) My Father is always at his work to this
very day, and I, too, am working.

John 5:17 (NIV)

SEPTEMBER 6th

Pride goeth before destruction,
and an haughty spirit before a fall.

Proverbs 16:18

SEPTEMBER 7th

If ye fulfil the royal law according to the scripture,
Thou shalt love thy neighbour as thyself, ye do well.

James 2:8

SEPTEMBER 8th

Seek ye first the kingdom of God, and his
righteousness; and all these things shall be
added unto you.

Matthew 6:33

SEPTEMBER 9th

Let us hold fast the profession of our faith without
wavering; (for he is faithful that promised).

Hebrews 10:23

SEPTEMBER 10th

He giveth power to the faint; and to them that have
no might he increaseth strength.

Isaiah 40:29

SEPTEMBER 11th

Live such good lives among the pagans that,
though they accuse you of doing wrong,
they may see your good deeds and glorify God.

1 Peter 2:12 (NIV)

SEPTEMBER 12th

Rejoice evermore. Pray without ceasing.
In every thing give thanks: for this is the will of God
in Christ Jesus concerning you.

1 Thessalonians 5:16-18

SEPTEMBER 13th

Having disarmed the powers and authorities,
(Jesus) made a public spectacle of them, triumphing
over them by the cross.

Colossians 2:15 (NIV)

SEPTEMBER 14th

He humbled himself, and became obedient unto
death, even the death of the cross. Wherefore God
hath highly exalted him.

Philippians 2:8-9

SEPTEMBER 15th

I will instruct thee and teach thee in the way which
thou shalt go: I will guide thee with mine eye.

Psalm 32:8

SEPTEMBER 16th

There is nothing covered, that shall not be revealed;
and hid, that shall not be known.

Matthew 10:26

SEPTEMBER 17th

Do not be overcome by evil,
but overcome evil with good.

Romans 12:21 (NIV)

SEPTEMBER 18th

Hereby perceive we the love of God, because he laid
down his life for us: and we ought to lay down our
lives for the brethren.

1 John 3:16

236

SEPTEMBER 19th

Godliness with contentment is great gain.

1 Timothy 6:6

SEPTEMBER 20th

Starting a quarrel is like breaching a dam;
so drop the matter before a dispute breaks out.

Proverbs 17:14 (NIV)

SEPTEMBER 21st

I am not come to call the righteous,
but sinners to repentance.

Matthew 9:13

SEPTEMBER 22nd

This is the day which the Lord hath made;
we will rejoice and be glad in it.

Psalm 118:24

SEPTEMBER 23rd

If ye love me, keep my commandments.

John 14:15

SEPTEMBER 24th

Let us come boldly unto the throne of grace,
that we may obtain mercy, and find grace to help
in time of need.

Hebrews 4:16

SEPTEMBER 25th

Now we see through a glass, darkly; but then face
to face: now I know in part; but then shall I know
even as I am known.

1 Corinthians 13:12

237

SEPTEMBER 26th

For the love of money is the root of all evil:
which while some have coveted after,
they have erred from the faith.

SEPTEMBER 27th

The name of the Lord is a strong tower:
the righteous runneth into it, and is safe.

Proverbs 18:10

SEPTEMBER 28th

Confess your faults one to another, and pray for
one another, that ye may be healed.

James 5:16

238

SEPTEMBER 29th

They overcame (Satan) by the blood of the Lamb,
and by the word of their testimony; and they loved
not their lives unto death.

Revelation 12:11

SEPTEMBER 30th

Water will gush forth in the wilderness and streams
in the desert. The burning sand will become a pool,
the thirsty ground bubbling springs.

Isaiah 35:6-7

OCTOBER 1st

Great and marvellous are thy works,
Lord God Almighty; just and true are thy ways,
thou King of all saints.

Revelation 15:3

OCTOBER 2nd

God commendeth his love toward us, in that,
while we were yet sinners, Christ died for us.

Romans 5:8

OCTOBER 3rd

Put on the whole armour of God, that ye may be able
to stand against the wiles of the devil.

Ephesians 6:11

OCTOBER 4th

He that loveth pleasure shall be a poor man;
he that loveth wine and oil shall not be rich.

Proverbs 21:17

OCTOBER 5th

We see Jesus, who was made a little lower than the
angels, now crowned with glory and honour because
he suffered death.

Hebrews 2:9 (NIV)

239

OCTOBER 6th

As the deer pants for streams of water, so my soul
pants for you, O God. My soul thirsts for God,
for the living God.

Psalm 42:1 (NIV)

OCTOBER 7th

Freely ye have received, freely give.

Matthew 10:8

OCTOBER 8th

Peacemakers who sow in peace raise a harvest
of righteousness.

James 3:18 (NIV)

240

OCTOBER 9th

Whatsoever ye do in word or deed,
do all in the name of the Lord Jesus,
giving thanks to God and the Father by him.

Colossians 3:17

OCTOBER 10th

In lowliness of mind let each esteem others better
than themselves.

Philippians 2:3

OCTOBER 11th

He who guards his mouth and his tongue keeps himself from calamity.

Proverbs 21:23 (NIV)

OCTOBER 12th

The word of God is quick, and powerful, and sharper than any two-edged sword... and is a discerner of the thoughts and intents of the heart.

Hebrews 4:12

OCTOBER 13th

As far as the east is from the west, so far hath he removed our transgressions from us.

Psalm 103:12

OCTOBER 14th

Do not repay evil for evil. Be careful to do what is right in the eyes of everybody.

Romans 12:17 (NIV)

OCTOBER 15th

How beautiful upon the mountains are the feet of him that bringeth good tidings...that saith unto Zion, Thy God reigneth!

Isaiah 52:7

OCTOBER 16th

I beseech you as strangers and pilgrims, abstain from fleshly lusts, which war against the soul.

1 Peter 2:11

OCTOBER 17th

Love does not delight in evil but rejoices with the truth. It always protects, always trusts, always hopes, always perseveres.

1 Corinthians 13:6-7 (NIV)

OCTOBER 18th

The harvest truly is great, but the labourers are few: pray ye therefore the Lord of the harvest, that he would send forth labourers into his harvest.

Luke 10:2

OCTOBER 19th

The Son of man came not to be ministered unto, but to minister, and to give his life a ransom for many.

Mark 9:45

OCTOBER 20th

Why art thou cast down, O my soul?
And why art thou disquieted within me?
Hope in God: for I shall yet praise him.

Psalm 43:5

OCTOBER 21st

A new commandment I give unto you,
That ye love one another as I have loved you.

John 13:34

OCTOBER 22nd

I have become all things to all men so that
by all possible means I might save some.

1 Corinthians 9:22

OCTOBER 23rd

Whoever loves money never has money enough;
whoever loves wealth is never satisfied with his
income. This too is meaningless.

Ecclesiastes 5:10 (NIV)

OCTOBER 24th

Ye are bought with a price: therefore glorify God
in your body, and in your spirit, which are God's.

1 Corinthians 6:20

OCTOBER 25th

Train up a child in the way that he should go:
and when he is old he will not depart from it.

Proverbs 22:6

OCTOBER 26th

I give unto them eternal life; and they shall never
perish, neither shall any man pluck them out of
my hand.

John 10:28

OCTOBER 27th

The Lord is not slow in keeping his promise...
He is patient with you, not wanting anyone to perish,
but everyone to come to repentance.

2 Peter 3:9 (NIV)

OCTOBER 28th

Ye are not of the world, but I have chosen you out
of the world; therefore the world hateth you.

John 15:19

OCTOBER 29th

As the heaven is high above the earth, so great
is his mercy toward them that fear him.

Psalm 103:11

OCTOBER 30th

Fight the good fight of faith, lay hold on eternal life,
whereunto thou art also called.

1 Timothy 6:12

OCTOBER 31st

An highway shall be there, and a way,
and it shall be called The way of holiness.

Isaiah 35:8

NOVEMBER 1st

Jesus said unto her, I am the resurrection, and the
life: he that believeth in me, though he were dead,
yet shall he live.

John 11:25

NOVEMBER 2nd

In his great mercy he has given us new birth into a
living hope... and into an inheritance that can never
perish, spoil or fade – kept in heaven for you.

1 Peter 1:3-4 (NIV)

NOVEMBER 3rd

Blessing, and glory, and wisdom, and thanksgiving, and honour, and power, and might, be unto our God for ever and ever. Amen.

Revelation 7:12

NOVEMBER 4th

There is therefore now no condemnation to them which are in Christ Jesus, who walk not after the flesh, but after the Spirit.

Romans 8:1

NOVEMBER 5th

Be ye doers of the word, and not hearers only, deceiving your own selves.

James 1:22

NOVEMBER 6th

We are God's workmanship, created in Christ Jesus to do good works, which God prepared in advance for us to do.

Ephesians 2:10

NOVEMBER 7th

Let the word of Christ dwell in you richly in all
wisdom; teaching and admonishing one another
in psalms and hymns and spiritual songs.

Colossians 3:16

NOVEMBER 8th

Give me neither poverty nor riches... lest I be full,
and deny thee, and say, Who is the Lord?
Or lest I be poor, and steal, and take the name
of my God in vain.

Proverbs 30:8-9

NOVEMBER 9th

"Come, follow me," Jesus said, "and I will make you
fishers of men."

Mark 1:17 (NIV)

NOVEMBER 10th

God is our refuge and strength, a very present help in
trouble. Therefore we will not fear, though the earth
be moved.

Psalm 46:1-2

NOVEMBER 11th

Ask and it shall be given you; seek and ye shall find;
knock and it shall be opened unto you.

Matthew 7:7

NOVEMBER 12th

Herein is love, not that we loved God, but that he
loved us, and sent his Son to be the propitiation for
our sins.

1 John 4:10

NOVEMBER 13th

Be careful that the exercise of your freedom does not
become a stumbling-block to the weak.

1 Corinthians 8:9 (NIV)

NOVEMBER 14th

He that giveth unto the poor shall not lack: but he
that hideth his eyes shall have many a curse.

Proverbs 28:27

NOVEMBER 15th

Remember those in prison as if you were their fellow-
prisoners, and those who are ill-treated as if you
yourselves were suffering.

Hebrews 13:3 (NIV)

NOVEMBER 16th

Let us draw near with a true heart in full assurance
of faith, having our hearts sprinkled from an evil
conscience.

Hebrews 10:22

NOVEMBER 17th

O sing unto the Lord a new song; for he hath done
marvellous things: his right hand, and his holy arm,
hath gotten him the victory.

Psalm 98:1

NOVEMBER 18th

Thou shalt love the Lord thy God with all they heart,
and with all thy soul, and with all thy mind, and
with all thy strength: this is the first commandment.

Mark 12:30

NOVEMBER 19th

Thou shalt love thy neighbour as thyself. There is
none other commandment greater than these.

Mark 12:31

ROBERT HICKS

NOVEMBER 20th

Be joyful in hope, patient in affliction, faithful in prayer.

Romans 12:12 (NIV)

NOVEMBER 21st

Jesus saith unto him, I am the way, the truth and the life: no man cometh unto the Father, but by me.

John 14:6

NOVEMBER 22nd

Sensible people will see trouble coming and avoid it, but an unthinking person will walk right into it and regret it later.

Proverbs 27:12 (GNB)

NOVEMBER 23rd

I am the Alpha and the Omega, the beginning and the ending, saith the Lord, which is, and which was, and which is to come, the Almighty.

Revelation 1:8

NOVEMBER 24th

(God) only is my rock and my salvation: he is my defence; I shall not be moved.

Psalm 62:6

NOVEMBER 25th

Be not forgetful to entertain strangers: for thereby
some have entertained angels unawares.

Hebrews 13:2

NOVEMBER 26th

Boast not thyself of tomorrow; for thou knowest
not what a day may bring forth.

Proverbs 27:1

NOVEMBER 27th

Now you are the body of Christ,
and each one of you is a part of it.

1 Corinthians 12:27 (NIV)

251

NOVEMBER 28th

They that wait upon the Lord shall renew their
strength...they shall run and not be weary;
and they shall walk, and not faint.

Isaiah 40:31

NOVEMBER 29th

The end of all things is near. Therefore be clear
minded and self-controlled, so that you can pray.

1 Peter 4:7 (NIV)

NOVEMBER 30th

Be careful, or your hearts will be weighed down with dissipation, drunkenness and the anxieties of life.

Luke 21:34

DECEMBER 1st

Be not conformed to this world, but be ye transformed by the renewing of your mind.

Romans 12:2

DECEMBER 2nd

Be strong in the Lord, and in the power of his might.

Ephesians 6:10

DECEMBER 3rd

Devote yourselves to prayer, being watchful and thankful.

Colossians 4:2 (NIV)

DECEMBER 4th

A bruised reed shall he not break, and the smoking flax shall he not quench.

Isaiah 42:3

DECEMBER 5th

The wisdom that comes from heaven is first of all pure, then peace-loving, considerate, submissive, full of mercy and good fruit, impartial and sincere.

James 3:17 (NIV)

DECEMBER 6th

Do not let your heart envy sinners, but always be zealous for the fear of the Lord.

Proverbs 23:17 (NIV)

DECEMBER 7th

He which hath begun a good work in you will perform it until the day of Jesus Christ.

Philippians 1:6

253

DECEMBER 8th

Restore us, O God Almighty; make your face shine upon us, that we may be saved.

Psalm 80:7 (NIV)

DECEMBER 9th

If ye then being evil know how to give good gifts unto your children, how much more will your Father which is in heaven give good things to them that ask him?

Matthew 7:11

DECEMBER 10th

For to me to live is Christ, and to die is gain.

Philippians 1:21

DECEMBER 11th

You are chosen people, a royal priesthood,
a holy nation, a people belonging to God;
that you may declare the praises of him who called
you out of darkness.

1 Peter 2:9 (NIV)

DECEMBER 12th

God is faithful, who will not suffer you to be tempted above that ye are able; but will with the temptation also make a way to escape.

1 Corinthians 10:13

DECEMBER 13th

An honest answer is like a kiss on the lips.

Proverbs 24:26

DECEMBER 14th

In everything by prayer and supplication
with thanksgiving let your requests be
made known to God.

Philippians 4:6

DECEMBER 15th

He that dwelleth in the secret place of the most High
shall abide under the shadow of the Almighty.

Psalm 91:1

255

DECEMBER 16th

Whatsoever ye shall ask in my name, that will I do,
that the Father may be glorified in the Son.

John 14:13

DECEMBER 17th

Be not drunk with wine, wherein is excess,
but be filled with the Spirit.

Ephesians 5:18

DECEMBER 18th

He who searches our hearts knows the mind of the
Spirit, because the Spirit intercedes for the saints in
accordance with God's will.

Romans 8:27 (NIV)

DECEMBER 19th

If thine enemy be hungry, give him bread to eat;
and if he be thirsty, give him water to drink.

Proverbs 25:21

DECEMBER 20th

Let us not give up meeting together, as some are in
the habit of doing, but let us encourage one another.

Hebrews 10:25 (NIV)

DECEMBER 21st

My soul doth magnify the Lord,
and my spirit hath rejoiced in God my saviour.

Luke 1:46-47

DECEMBER 22nd

O come, let us worship and bow down: let us kneel
before the Lord our maker. For he is our God:
and we are the people of his pasture and the sheep
of his hand.

Psalm 95:6-7

DECEMBER 23rd

When the time had fully come, God sent forth his
Son, 'born of a woman, born under law, to redeem
those under law, that we might receive the full rights
of sons.

Galatians 4:4-5 (NIV)

DECEMBER 24th

Blessed be the Lord God of Israel;
for he hath visited and redeemed his people.

Luke 1:68

257

DECEMBER 25th

And the Word was made flesh, and dwelt among us,
(and we beheld his glory, the glory as of the only
begotten of the Father,) full of grace and truth.

John 1:14

DECEMBER 26th

I rejoice at thy word, as one that findeth great spoil.
I hate and abhor lying: but thy law do I love.

Psalm 119:162-163

DECEMBER 27th

This then is the message which we have heard of
him, and declare to you, that God is light, and in him
is no darkness at all.

1 John 1:5

DECEMBER 28th

God hath chosen the foolish things of the world to
confound the wise; and God hath chosen the weak
things of the world to confound those things which
are mighty.

1 Corinthians 1:27

DECEMBER 29th

Do not answer a fool according to his folly,
or you will be like him yourself.

Proverbs 26:4 (NIV)

DECEMBER 30th

Worthy is the Lamb that was slain to receive power, and riches, and wisdom, and strength, and honour, and glory, and blessing.

Revelation 5:12

DECEMBER 31st

The Lord reigneth, he is clothed with majesty; the Lord is clothed with strength... the world also is established, that it cannot be moved.

Psalm 93:1

SLUMS TO
BUCKINGHAM PALACE

SLUMS TO BUCKINGHAM PALACE

I now wish to highlight a few comments, again of a personal nature.

ANNABELLE

Following the transfer of Joyce to Heaven, I subsequently married an amazing lady who was relaxed to be single, yet was prepared to take me on! Many friends of her family told me at the time how fortunate I was to be marrying Annabelle!. The subsequent years have demonstrated how correct was their judgment!

EMILY-ROSE

Unexpectedly, a few years later another joy came into our lives, all wrapped up into one little girl, now fast growing into a young lady – Emily-Rose.

BUCKINGHAM PALACE

It was with Annabelle and Emily-Rose that I made a trip to London near the end of the year of Her Majesty's Golden Jubilee Year, to present at Buckingham Palace a copy of a Bible. It was the same

'King James' 350-year-old translation of the Bible that I had copied out by hand!

400 YEARS: 50 YEARS: ONE BIBLE

While our Queen Elizabeth the Second was celebrating 50 years on the throne, it was the 400th Anniversary of King James the First had ascended to the throne (following the death of Elizabeth the First), and in that first year of his reign he initiated the translation of the Bible which would thereafter bear his name.

So, it seemed fitting that Her Majesty the Queen should receive a new copy of the 'King James' Bible.

With a publishing friend, David Wavre, we had completely together arranged for the re-typesetting of the King James Bible, and bringing the page layout up to date for the 21st Century.

It was a joy to be with David, as we passed through the gates of Buckingham Palace.

As Emily-Rose headed off across the Palace Forecourt, I called her back to walk more slowly and take in the atmosphere of being on the inside of those famous railings. I realised this may not happen again in her lifetime! Tourists on the outside, were taking pictures of anything and everyone that moved on the inside, including ourselves!

COMMEMORATIVE BIBLE GOSPELS

Following our time at the Palace, we then had another duty to perform because I was also presenting a Bible to Mr. Charles Moore, Editor of the national broadsheet, "The Daily Telegraph".

It was "The Daily Telegraph" who had encouraged the national initiative of the commemoration Bible Gospels for the Millennium 2000, which resulted in the largest printing of Bible Gospels in recorded history with around 5,000,000 being distributed in 10,000 churches and communities in the United Kingdom through the involvement of hundreds of thousands of Christians, to mark 2000 years of Christianity A further 2-3,000,000 Millennium Gospels were also sent to 'developing countries'.

265

A GREAT HONOUR

While in the office of Charles Moore, arrangements had been made for a portrait of myself to be presented to Birmingham University. The portrait had been done by Henry Mee, who has painted portraits of Her Majesty the Queen and other Royals, Prime Ministers and other distinguished individuals. The portrait was handed over to Professor Michael Clark who received it on behalf of the University. Later, I would have the privilege of seeing it on display in the private office of the Chancellor of the University prior to it being hung in the entrance to the Student Library with a brief testimony of my life to inspire present students.

The University now includes the buildings which in the 1950's had been an Institution for the Care & Protection of Children, and where I and some of my siblings had lived at different times. As you can imagine, I found all this amazing and humbling, and yet somehow fitting as a testimony to the fact that the Bible is a Miracle Book.

A 'MIRACLE BOOK' FOR MILLIONS

Although my own encounter with the Bible was unusual and exceptional, I have met hundreds of individuals to whom the same Bible is also a Miracle Book. I am aware of thousands, even millions, who have discovered this simply by opening its pages and developing a regular habit of reading, even small sections of the most amazing Book in the history of the world.

Undoubtedly it is the most amazing book – but Christians believe it is more than that. We really do believe it is the 'Word of God'. Each society which distances itself from this exceptional Book, soon becomes the poorer for that.

So, I close this Gift Book with a simple but very real conclusion.

The miracle of the Bible is available to us 'all, irrespective of our background, makeup, education or position in life ... and the proof this statement is readily available and easy to put to the test.

IT'S FOR YOU, ALSO

Today, we have more Bibles, beautifully produced, beautifully designed and in modern English, many with useful notes to help the understanding. I am often asked, "What is the best way to read the Bible?" "A bit and often," is my response. "A Chapter, or part of a Chapter, on a regular basis, and then occasionally a good long read." I have found this works for most folk, although of course there are some individuals for whom reading comes easily and they can take larger portions. I have known many individuals who have developed the habit of reading through the entire Bible year by year. In actual fact, it only takes 15-20 minutes each day to achieve this. However, my advice to most individuals remains, "A bit and often."

Again and again, Bible-reading individuals have told me that slowly but surely a miracle begins to take place in their own appreciation of this wonderful Book and, in time, they recognise that the 'Miracle Book' is in fact what a previous generation called, "The Good Book" and "The Word of God". Whether you are a slow reader or a fast one, an extensive or a casual one,

I encourage you to read this marvellous Book for yourself.

I do hope this book from the man who once was the boy-with-his-Bible will be an encouragement to you.

BEFORE I CLOSE

BEFORE I CLOSE

I realise that I have only given the minimum events in my life that covered the period from 1956 to the publishing of this book.

Part of the reason is that the sequel to "A Child Cries" – the story of my first fifteen years – covers my early and mid-adult years in greater detail, leading up to my wife's death and the impact of that bereavement.

The main reason, however, is that this book is designed simply to raise awareness in the greatest Book of all time – the Holy Bible.

Having lived the way I have, and having met numerous folk from all walks of life, I have reached – as you would expect – a range of convictions concerning the impact of what I call the "Miracle Book" on individual lives.

Most people tend to identify themselves as 'ordinary' – although that is not God's description of them. The media then elevates certain individuals to a 'celebrity' status, and then plagues them with criticism or intrusion – or even both at the same time.   Such 'celebrities' tend to come from the entertainment industry of music, films, television and sport.

However, whether you are a 'celebrity' or an 'ordinary' person, you will find within you the same need as me for personal worth and well-being. It is from my own experience that I have therefore come to the following affirmations.

ONE

Firstly, we all have needs that are larger on the inside, than can be satisfied by the world with all its 'razz-ma-tazz' and drama on the outside.

TWO

Secondly, the 'Miracle Book' when absorbed 'little and often' with an open heart, will correspond to the vacuum within us of many needs.

THREE

Thirdly, in time, we will discover that Jesus Christ is not only the Son of God but has brought into being a 'New Humanity', that is now available to each one of us individually. This new humanity meets the great need of nations, cities, town and villages, small communities, right down to families and individuals. This new humanity is based on doing what is right, and doing it with love, until faith, hope and love become not only worthy virtues to live up to, but living attributes blended into who and what we are.

FOUR

The reality of this new humanity came about by the death and resurrection of Jesus Christ. The evil and curse that has spoiled so much in this world and also within each of us individually, decreases, and eventually is banished, when we have a friendship with Jesus and as the spiritual side of our being – the huge void within us – becomes filled.

FIVE

The fifth affirmation is that the local church is still the best 'Institution' that allows our own Christian faith to grow and develop.

273

These basic persuasions, that can be counted on one hand, I would commend to anyone reading this book.

For myself, the Holy Bible became in my teens my 'Miracle Book'. During the subsequent years of growth and development, I have made many mistakes - or to use the Bible expression, I have "sinned" many times – yet I can still testify that after all these years, the Holy Bible is still my "Miracle Book".

I also am amazed!

Was it really true
That the streetboy, the ragamuffin, the gutter kid

ROBERT HICKS

Would one day visit Buckingham Palace
With the same Bible he had copied out by hand
When its words were already 350 years old
And for the Golden Jubilee of Her Majesty the Queen
It was 400 years old?

How can this book-
That took over 1500 years to write
And was completed 2000 years ago
    – Change the life of a boy from the slums?

Yet this is the testimony,
Not only of one boy,
But of millions and millions throughout the centuries
And it could be the testimony of you as you read this
    book today.